From Plato's Cave to the Multiplex

From Plato's Cave to the Multiplex
Contemporary Philosophy and Film

Edited by

Barbara Gabriella Renzi and Stephen Rainey

CAMBRIDGE SCHOLARS PRESS

From Plato's Cave to the Multiplex: Contemporary Philosophy and Film, edited by Barbara Gabriella Renzi and Stephen Rainey

This book first published 2006 by

Cambridge Scholars Press

15 Angerton Gardens, Newcastle, NE5 2JA, UK

British Library Cataloguing in Publication Data
A catalogue record for this book is available from the British Library

ISBN 1-84718-013-2

TABLE OF CONTENTS

PREFACE

Two years ago I wrote a brief preface to a collection of essays edited by the philosophy postgraduate research students of Queen's University Belfast. These essays issued from an international conference for philosophy postgraduates organised here in Belfast in spring 2004. It secured the participation of 40 researchers from several countries, and eight of the contributions were published in the volume entitled Noesis.. In that preface I referred to the support of senior staff at the students' conference, which should be seen as reciprocating the support which the students themselves had lent to the Joint Session and associated conferences during a week of Philosophiefest at Queen's in July 2003. Those events depended crucially for their success on the students, who were in turn inspired to try their own hand at conference organisation.

The wheel continues to turn. In November 2005 an important conference on medieval philosophy was organised by the seniors with important assistance from our research students in that area. Now we have the publication of a second volume of essays by the same publishers, Scholars Press of Cambridge, who facilitated Noesis. From Plato's Cave to the Multiplex, with ten papers selected from a larger range and the same geographical spread of participants, connects themes in the mainstream of philosophy and its history with the interests of mass culture, as expressed in film.

What is the relationship between the world as it is found in and through artistic portrayal and the world which precedes such portrayal and stands independent of it? Answers vary from the robust realism of Plato as traditionally construed – that art can at best imitate reality to the metaphysical disadvantage of art, to a postmodern insistence on the primacy and autonomy of the created reality. Kant, Hegel and Marx occupy positions somewhat intermediate between these extremes; and even the realism of the traditional Plato is much questioned by contemporary hermeneutical studies of his works.

So this is an area of philosophical debate in which there is everything to play for. Our contributors do so with vigour and rigour. I commend their work to your inspection.

David Evans

INTRODUCTION

Most books that offer an introduction to philosophy usually begin with a chapter that attempts to explain what philosophy *is*. More often than not, these attempts purposely arrive at no definition. Philosophy, the newcomer is left to suppose, is a vague notion.

The resistance to definition that philosophy embodies occurs often enough to produce at least puzzlement in the reader, and at most consternation; if you can't say what it is, then what's the point in taking it up? To counter such an attitude, all that would be needed is some accessible medium whereby philosophical thought, problems and ideas could be portrayed in such a way as to provoke philosophical thinking merely through engaging with the medium.

With film, this task is fulfilled. The key to the simultaneously accessible yet provocative nature of film lies in the possibilities of interpretation. Most well made cinema can be watched passively, as a simple piece of entertainment. Or again, it can be viewed more actively, perhaps with conscious attention to the motives, intentions and techniques of the director. And again, it can be viewed as a fixed context wherein problems and solutions arise within a closed, fictional world, or as a starting point or catalyst for reflection. The possibilities are endless.

When the endless possibilities of the medium are combined with the intentions of a philosophically informed director, film can really stand as philosophy; film can be considered philosophy in itself, or as the matter for philosophical discussion.

This book then is written with the idea in mind that some films can do more than just illustrate philosophical questions. Utilising both mainstream and art house production some chapters in this book show that films produce philosophical points on their own: films can work *as* philosophy, rather than insights into the film being gained through philosophy. Other chapters identify well known philosophical positions, arguments and issues that are presented or exemplified through films. We are aware of the fact that with ingenuity it is easy to identify philosophical issues in any film, as Des O'Rawe, from the Film Studies domain, reminds us in his *Afterword*. However it is undeniable that some films are more philosophical than others and need less ingenuity for such identification. It is just thoughts like these that lie behind this collection of papers. Real philosophical problems and positions are presented and elucidated with central reference to movies, and filmmaking generally. Films like *Fight*

Club and *Lost in Translation* meet the philosophical tides of positivism and feminism, while the Heideggerean heart of *The Thin Red Line* is exposed just as Hume's likely thoughts on the horror genre are revealed.

A brief word on the course the book takes will be followed by a more detailed introduction to each chapter.

The first chapter in this collection establishes many of the themes that are to be pursued throughout the book as a whole. Geoffrey Hill's examination of David Fincher's *Fight Club* raises questions about the nature of the self and identity, while more generally problematising the nature of known reality. The themes of self and other are focussed upon in Jolynna Sinanan's Heideggerean reading of Terence Malick's *Thin Red Line*. In each case, great philosophical mileage can be had from these extremely well known modern pieces of cinema.

In each of the opening chapters, some discussion is made of the technical decisions that directors make in order to establish points of interest or insight. It is clear that, in philosophically-minded filmmaking in particular, the directorial agenda can drive the philosophical issues. This theme is explicitly explored both in Orna Raviv's discussion of the close-up and in John Adams' dissection of Robert Bresson's attitude toward filmmaking *per se*. What's more, in these discussions it becomes clear that for the directors under scrutiny, the audience features in the thought process over and above the making of a film. The audience is actively considered as the director attempts to create moments on screen, either through the immediacy of identity in the case of close-up, or the evocation of empathy in Bresson. On this theme, Mark C. Rainey explores the possibly puzzling motivation that would lead cinema-goers to actively seek out that which ought to repulse.

The ethical possibilities of film are raised in John F. Catherwood's discussion of the moral implications and positions shown in Frank Capra's *It's a Wonderful Life*. In a synthesis of these themes, the audience and ethics, Catherine Wheatley explores the ethical relation between the audience and film with reference to Kantian ethics and the films of Michael Haneke.

The Kantian ethical theme is pursued and extended to include reference to Marxism in Barbara Renzi's discussion of *I Girasoli* (*Sunflowers*) and *La Classe Operaia va in Paradiso* (*The Working Class go to Heaven*) in which the characters have themselves subjected to various moral and practical problems. Lucy Bolton's discussion of Sophia Coppola's *Lost in Translation* draws together many of the themes present in the preceding chapters to give a wide-ranging discussion of cinematic portrayals (hence identity of self and other), filmic techniques and directorial audience-consciousness with specific reference to feminist theory. Finally, Stephen Rainey discusses the epistemological character of cinema in that the matter of cinema in general is assessed in terms of its fundamental *noetic* import.

***

Geoffrey Hill examines David Fincher's *Fight Club* of 1999 through the lens of nineteenth century positivist philosophy. Hill notes the changing aesthetic of late twentieth century filmmaking, with its emphasis upon more and more realistic depiction of its fictive constructs. Ironically, the march of technology makes this realistic aesthetic increasingly realisable through ever more clever digital constructions. The tension between the real and the constructed is what motivates Hill's examination in this piece. Theorists and thinkers of the nineteenth century, in trying to explain the world, could be seen as falling into two camps. In one camp was Thomas Hardy, who thought of reality as that which underwrites any reading we hope to make of events. Reality is something 'other', while the fancies of our minds are mere attempts at evasion of this monolithic and unchangeable reality. Meanwhile, thinkers in the other camp, such as George Eliot, were more optimistic about the power of the mind, and less in awe of transcendent reality. For Eliot, the mind had the power to transform reality, either by way of our own valuations, or by informed intervention. This nineteenth century tension surfaces remarkably clearly in the struggle of *Fight Club*'s nameless narrator as he struggles between the brute nature of reality and the transformative power of his alter ego, Tyler Durden. Hill's interpretation offers a challenge to the prevalent reading of *Fight Club* as being centrally concerned with issues of violence and misogyny.

Jolynna Sinanan's discussion of *The Thin Red Line* convincingly argues that Terence Malick's creation is actually intended to show the thought of Martin Heidegger on film. She explores the characterisations, messages and techniques Malick encodes and uses in his work through the lens of Heidegger's notion of 'Dasein' and that of 'authenticity'. Her Heideggerean elucidation of this war film show it to be more than it seems; an exploration of war, life, death, self and otherness and humanity, all expertly rendered on film by the philosophically insightful mind of Malick. In short, Sinanan convincingly shows Malick's *Thin Red Line* to be 'possibly the most profound war movie of the post world war two era'.

Orna Raviv's chapter links the challenging thought of Emmanuel Levinas to the cinematic medium, putting great emphasis upon the ethical dimension of 'the Other'. In particular, Raviv is keen to show the link between Levinas' idea of the Other as another person, and the face as a transcendental object in which the Other appears *as another person.* With keen insight into the history and mechanics of filmmaking, Raviv gives a historical exploration of the close-up and explains its changing role throughout the history of filmmaking. The ultimate role of the close-up, Raviv argues, is to create a cinematic moment unlike any other in experience; the identification of the Other without rational appraisal; the pure perception of Otherness in the face of the Other. Using precise language and sources, Raviv's appealing paper gives a clear and enlightening account of a very rarefied and challenging philosophical position.

John Adams' concern is with the, let's say, atypical filmmaking of Robert Bresson. Bresson's approach to film is to suppress precisely what might be thought of as the most essential elements of film *per se*, namely acting, direction and soundtrack. Bresson describes the vast majority of film pejoratively as 'filmed theatre'. Adams' endeavour is to explain Bresson's attitude and his motivation. We also see another alternative conception of film, provided in contra-distinction, in the person of Andrei Tarkovsky. The role of 'models' as opposed to actors is explained, as is Bresson's conception of film as nothing but the relation of objects to one another according to a director's vision. The director's vision is everything that's required to make a moment. In this way, as Adams notes, for Bresson in film 'everything is necessary. All in all, we are left with a clearly explained alternative conception of what film is according to Bresson.

Mark C. Rainey updates David Hume's essay *On Tragedy* in assessing the status of what has come to be known as 'the paradox of horror'. Since, for Hume, we are motivated by the desire for pleasure and the avoidance of pain, why on earth would we ever subject ourselves to the horrific sights and sounds of (well made) horror movies? How can we be said to *enjoy the horrific* unless we ourselves are monsters? Never fear; Rainey's clear discussion of the arguments will set your mind at ease, so you may watch *The Ring* in peace. Having surveyed the arguments on each side of the contemporary debate, Rainey gives his own view, at the same time as presenting a filmography well worth working through!

John Catherwood sets out to challenge the received notion of Frank Capra's *It's a Wonderful Life* as merely a feel-good, Christmas movie. In doing so, he also goes against the supposition that the film stands as a utilitarian fairy tale, or something of that sort. This challenge is mounted by careful attention to the intellectual underpinnings of the many of the variously interpretable messages portrayed in the film. The utilitarian interpretation of Capra's work is closely critiqued and challenged on several points of substance, not least in terms of the documented moral position of Capra himself and his ideology of 'one man, one film'. The thesis is advanced that *It's a Wonderful Life* is really a complicated portrayal of Capra's own feelings regarding personal worth; it is a complex portrayal as it is a complex issue. Competing themes such as one's role in the community, one's individual actions and one's response to circumstances all factor in to a conception of moral worth as something revolving around the individual within a network of happy and willing friends. A wonderful life it may be, then, but not because an ethical calculus deems it so.

Catherine Wheatley discusses the films of Michael Haneke with respect to Kantian rational agency and ethics. This is a considerable shift in emphasis in a discussion of ethics and film, since it is the role of the audience and not the on-screen antics that are primarily being considered. Wheatley deftly locates her subject matter by distinguishing between 'moralist critics', whose concern is with the hermetically sealed moral world of a cinematic work, and 'political modernism', which focuses on the possibly coercive political nature of film. Each approach is lacking, and Wheatley offers the moral thinking of Kant as a superior viewpoint from which to consider the ethical implications of being an audience. Furthermore, we are shown how the films of Michael Haneke contain a particular challenge for the ethics and film theorist. His work sits between the two 'standard models' of 'realist filmmaking' and the reactionary 'counter-cinema' movement. Indeed, Wheatley notes that even Haneke himself considered that, when watching one of his movies, walking out might be the only morally responsible thing to do.

Barbara Renzi's wide-ranging paper begins with a general outline of Kant's ethical philosophy which provides the backdrop for a discussion of the Italian film, *Sunflowers*. This film, Renzi maintains, exemplifies Kantian morality in action as the recognition of the necessity of certain actions under the concept of duty motivates the characters throughout the plot, even though this sometimes conflicts with desire satisfaction. Duty, more than anything else, motivates the characters in *Sunflowers*. Given Kant's view of freedom, that free action is that done by free will, hence in accord with duty, the protagonists in *Sunflowers* are free. In marked contrast with this is the predicament of the main character in *The Working Class goes to Heaven*. Renzi's discussion of this film shows clearly how the Marxist notion of alienation can come about in the worker. As the main character, Lulù, becomes a better and better worker, he becomes less and less the man he once was. He becomes more like the cogs and levers of the machine he operates than a real human being. This spiritual de-humanisation of Lulù is only brought home to him once he is physically injured in the workplace. His instrumental compromise leads to a realisation of himself as more than a machine, and precipitates a move to join the activities of Leftists. After this epiphany, Lulù sees his work very differently, illustrating one major facet of Marxist thought extremely starkly.

Lucy Bolton presents the feminist thought of Luce Irigaray in terms of Sofia Coppola's 2003 release, *Lost in Translation*. Irigaray's feminism could be termed a feminism of essential difference, as opposed to that associated with Simone de Beauvoir. Bolton clearly explains how the societal role of women in 'phallocentric' cultures plays down 'interiority' in women and emphasises the exterior. Women are objects, seductresses or merely superficial. Generally, this societal stereotype is played out too in film. Coppola's film is an exception, however, and Bolton argues persuasively for the characteristically female nature of the film. Charlotte is clearly central in the film. And not only is this the case, but in the depiction of her silence, thoughts and unarticulated musings, her 'inner life' is placed centre stage. Unlike many standard portrayals of women in mainstream cinema (to which ironic reference is made throughout the film) Coppola presents Charlotte as a woman with a mind of her own, who can stand alone. In this, and the intricacies Bolton explains in terms of Irigarayan feminism, *Lost in Translation* is shown to be 'subtly revolutionary'.

Stephen Rainey's piece adopts the metaphor of the cave, as used by Plato in his *Republic*, and looks at how the experience of going to the movies can be related to this Platonic imagine. Plato's general thoughts regarding the role of truth are outlined, before the role of the audience with respect to cinematic knowledge is discussed. A central issue in Rainey's work is, in fact, whether an account of cinematic knowledge can be given. What results is a possibly worrying (to realists at least) critique of cinematic knowledge based upon the metaphor of the point of view, and a challenge to the realist assumption of 'cosmic exile'.

****

Special thanks are due to Professor David Evans, Dr Alan Weir, Mr Christopher McKnight whose attendance at several of the papers, and chairing various sessions was much appreciated. Thanks also to Mary Emmerson, secretary of the School of Philosophical Studies, whose help and advice was invaluable, and to Giulio Napolitano.

CHAPTER ONE

RADICAL REALITIES: BRITISH NINETEENTH-CENTURY POSITIVISM AND FICTIVE MENTAL CONSTRUCTIONS IN THE FILM *FIGHT CLUB*

GEOFFREY HILL

In the Hollywood films of the late twentieth-century we find a new realist aesthetic that bears a striking resemblance to the realism espoused by the positivism of the late 1800's. With technological advances in film Hollywood has been about the business of trying to make their fictive constructions appear more and more life-like. At the same time that films could be said to reproduce "reality" more and more accurately (but arguably less and less faithfully), the very things that produce these realities - special effects - are computer generated. In this new model fancy and imagination are employed to produce a radical reality of sorts where the false-ness of the construction is celebrated and highlighted instead of hidden or suppressed as it was in a certain brand of British Nineteenth-century positivism.

The manner in which positivism dealt with the problem of reconciling "the biological and the moral" can tell us a great deal about how Fight Club (1999) attempts to reconcile fictive mental constructions with the actuality of the world. For positivism,

> [e]ventually [...] the problem is resolved by what amounts to a bifurcation of the positivist camp into logical positivists, who [...] simply exclude moral questions from philosophy proper and pragmatists, who reinterpret the concept of philosophy itself so that it becomes no longer the pursuit of truth or reality but, in Richard Rorty's phrase, "a tool for coping with reality".[1]

In the film, the nameless protagonists attempt to cope with reality comes into direct conflict with late twentieth-century Hollywood's pursuit of realism (or "truth").

---

[1] Dale (1989), p. 21.

What we find in the film Fight Club, then, can be better understood when considered in the context of positivist philosophy. The departure from actuality we find in Fight Club, finds its progenitor in "positivism ['s] depart[ure] from the criterion of verification".[2] As positivism grappled with how it would deal with the actuality of the world that it was presented two divergent philosophies emerged. These two philosophies are expressed in the writings of numerous literary and philosophical figures of the time, but I am particularly interested in how these philosophies are expressed by George Eliot and Thomas Hardy. According to Peter Allan Dale, Hardy saw the "mind's constructions as imaginary evasions of a natural reality we fear to confront and cannot possibly alter",[3] while George Eliot "falls back on an arbitrary valuation of our mental images [...] and on the confidence that they can eventually remake the real, that they have the energy to change whatever nature has given us, externally or in the self".[4] The tension between these two philosophies of the imagination help articulate or describe the internal struggle of the nameless protagonist that leads to the psychotic doubling and the creation of his alter ego (Tyler Durden).

The psychology represented or depicted in the film is, as Dale argues of early psychoanalysis in general, "no less derivative from the root of nineteenth-century positivism".[5] The type of doubling that is found in Fight Club is a product or result of the type of radical reality offered by the filmic imaginary that, again, finds its roots in British Nineteenth-century Positivism. This doubling is a pathology of sorts. Henry Giroux has argued that pathology is central to the film, but for Giroux,

> The pathology at issue, [...] the one [...] central to *Fight Club*, is [the film's] intensely misogynist representation of women, and its intimation that violence is the only means through which men can be cleansed of the dire affect women have on the shaping of their identities. From the first scene of *Fight Club* to the last, women are cast as the binary opposite of masculinity. Women are both the other and a form of pathology. Jack begins his narrative by claiming that Marla is the cause of all his problems.[6]

That pathology - any condition that is a deviation from the normal - is a significant theme in the film is undoubtedly the case. However, I differ with Giroux as to which pathology is central. Giroux's description of the female as a

---

[2] *Ibid*, p. 281.
[3] *Ibid,* p. 282.
[4] *Ibid.*, p. 282.
[5] *Ibid.*, p. 281.
[6] Giroux (2000), pp. 37-38.

form of pathology is consistent with the tenor of the majority of critical scholarship treating *Fight Club*.

Recent critical engagement of the film Fight Club has constituted variations on the themes of masculinity - violence, homophobia, misogyny - and (anti) consumerism. Critics such as Henry Giroux have argued that the film represents an "attack on capitalism and consumerism",[7] but is only successful in reinscribing the systems and structures it supposedly criticizes. He writes, "Fight Club ultimately manages to offer a critique of the social and political conditions produced by contemporary capitalism only in a way that confirms capitalism's worst excesses and legitimates its ruling narratives". There are two significant blind spots in this type of treatment of the film that I would like to address. These blind spots also highlight the radical reality and link to positivist philosophy that I am trying to describe. First, there is no film analysis offered. By this I mean that at no point does Giroux explain how the film accomplishes the things he claims it does (i.e. how framing, composition, camera technique, sound, and editing visualize and communicate how we are supposed to see the film). What does the film communicate via visuals and sound? In some cases the shots and sound in the film make Giroux's statements problematic or even challenge them outright. (A point I will return to below). Second, if as Giroux claims, the film operates as a "public pedagogy that articulates knowledge to effects, purposely attempting to influence how and what knowledge and identities can be produced within a range of limited social relations".[8] He fails to address what models are available for the self-made individual to follow.

What follows are brief analyses of several key moments in the film that are intended to demonstrate the function I attribute to psychotic doubling as well as the radical realism that both creates and supports this type (model) of re-fashioning, thus exposing it as false.

The first is the scene in which the nameless protagonist returns from a trip to find his apartment and all of his worldly possessions blown to pieces. The manner in which the apartment complex sign is visually presented is significant. In the establishing shot of the scene the viewer is shown the sign in front of the apartment building, which reads "Pearson Towers, A Place To Be Somebody", for a split second before the camera pans away. As the nameless protagonist is coming home from the airport the sign is centred in the frame (in the foreground) and zoomed in on rather close. We see his cab approaching in the background and the camera pans quickly to follow the cab until it stops. As this is being presented visually we hear the nameless protagonist say, "Home was a

---

[7] *Ibid.*, p. 41.
[8] *Ibid.*, p. 39.

condo on the fifteenth floor of a filing cabinet for widows and young professionals" (Fight Club 25:46 - 25:50). The intended contradiction is rather obvious - particularly if one notices the sign. It is a place to be nobody, emblematic of there being no "real" identity to be found. Here the residence of the NP becomes a physical representation of his mental state of being. This keys us into the significance of psychology in the film.

The nameless protagonist has moved beyond what Freud considers the normal neurosis of splitting to psychotic doubling, where the unity of the ego breaks down and develops multiple personalities that exist independently of one another and may not communicate. For Freud (and Lacan), splitting is a necessary stage that takes on a normalizing function in the maturation process. In Fight Club psychotic doubling takes on the normalizing function of splitting and becomes part of the maturation process for the nameless protagonist, largely due to the privileging of the imagination over reality which is both allowed for and supported by the radical realism of late twentieth-century film.

The narrator creates an alter ego that allows him simultaneously to work as an ordinary person - a "recall coordinator" - and brutally beat people in the underground bare knuckles fight club that he initiates. This type of doubling is fundamentally different than examples in film from earlier in the twentieth century such as Taxi Driver where Travis Bickle (Robert De Niro) remakes himself into a celebrated vigilante hero. Bickle is all too aware of the identity change that he is effecting and goes about remaking himself in a conscious methodical manner, literally refashioning himself as he fashions his homemade weapons.

One reason that the NP begins to experience doubling has to do with his wish to dissociate himself from his day-to-day existence. He cannot reconcile this existence with his virtual self-image. This wish is not a new development. It is the technological developments in movie making which have led to a certain type of radical realism that allows a different type of dissociation to take the place of splitting and leads directly to the formation of a functional second self. The conflict between these two competing selves is emblematic of the conflict between the nameless protagonist's fictive mental constructions and the actuality of the world.

Next I will consider a speech delivered by Tyler Durden, referred to as "the middle children of history speech," that is a prime example of how the film can be misread if shots, framing, etc., are not taken into consideration. The speech occurs in the basement of Lou's tavern where the fight club meets to have their fights. The men have circled around Tyler and he begins his speech:

> Man, I see in fight club the strongest and smartest man who've ever lived. I see all this potential, and I see it squandered. Goddamn it an entire generation

pumping gas and waiting tables, slaves with white collars. Advertising has us chasing cars and clothes, working jobs we hate so we can buy shit we don't need. We're the middle children of history man, no purpose or place. We have no great war, no great depression. Our great war is a spiritual war. Our great depression is our lives. We've all been raised on television to believe that one day we'd all be millionaires and movie gods and rock stars - but we won't. And we're slowly learning that fact and we're very, very pissed off.[9]

What critics, such as Giroux and others, have focused on in this speech is Tyler's discussion of our being slaves to our jobs. The speech is peppered with anti-consumerism, but this is not all there is to be found. This also can be misread as the argument that the culture industry - of which the cinema is undoubtedly a part - is responsible for the commodification of every possible thing and space. Giroux goes on to say that Brad Pitt playing TD (in light of this speech especially) is "a contradiction that can't be overlooked" - but then does not address it himself. An important question is not asked: Is the star framed here as a mass commodity? (Yes) Here it would seem that how things are visually presented on the screen challenges outright Giroux's statements concerning what it means. The contradiction is clearly intended.

We should also pay attention to the bookends of the speech. Tyler begins by saying that he sees the strongest and smartest men that have ever lived in fight club. This is not simply a gross overstatement. It is meant to highlight, as the director David Fincher discusses in his commentary on the film (included in the DVD), that every individual we meet that has joined fight club is a "moron". Joining fight club is not going to help things and if anything it is the fight club, not women, that retards any possible productive movement. This scene is not simply an attempt to deal with trauma by returning to an earlier form of male culture as Giroux and others have it. It exposes this as not being the answer. Here the film may not signal the call to a return to a male, misogynistic culture but quite the opposite. This is not to say that the film is entirely successful in accomplishing this goal. However, that a film is not entirely successful in its aim does not mean that it simply reinscribes that which it is criticizing. We might want to ask what kind of work the director intends to be done by having one of THE movie gods of our time deliver this speech. This scene also sets up the trajectory of nameless protagonist's struggle to refashion himself. He cannot keep himself in the dark forever and rapidly moves toward an unavoidable confrontation of his alter ego.

---

[9] (1:09:46 - 1:11:16)

In what I call the confrontation scene the nameless protagonist (NP) asks Tyler why people keep mistaking the two of them for each other. To which his response to himself is:

> NP: Because we are the same person...Tyler, I don't understand this.
> TD: You were looking for a way to change your life, you could not do this on your own. All the ways you WISH you could be, that's me. I look like you want to look, I fuck like you want to fuck, I am smart, capable, and most importantly I am free in all the ways that you are not...
> NP: No, this impossible, this is crazy...
> TD: People do it every day. They talk to themselves and they see themselves as they would like to be, they don't have the courage you have to just run with it. Naturally you are still wrestling with it so sometimes you're still you...other times you imagine yourself watching me...little by little you're just letting yourself become Tyler Durden.(Fight Club, 1:53:03 - 1:54:04)

In looking for a way to change himself the nameless protagonist creates not just an alter ego, but a dream world to go with it. He begins to live more and more in the dream world of his imagination [as he privileges the imaginary over actuality] where his alter ego is all the ways he wishes he could be. This is an illusion cannot be sustained. Here we see the conflict between Hardy's philosophy that the minds constructions are imaginary evasions, "a natural reality that we fear to confront and cannot possible alter," and George Eliot's belief that our mental images can eventually remake the real, "that the have the energy to change whatever nature has given us, externally or in the self," come to a head (no pun intended). The nameless protagonist very much wants to believe that his mental images can remake the real and change both what is both external and within himself, but at the same time undoubtedly fears confronting reality (himself) and creates imaginary evasions (mental images) to this end. This seemingly irresolvable conflict leads to the psychotic doubling that we find in the film and eventually to the confrontation scene outlined above. It is this scene that forces the nameless protagonist to recognize the crossovers that have been occurring for quite some time.

Hints of these crossovers appear throughout the film and are too numerous to enumerate here. One of the forms in which these hints appear is single images of Tyler Durden "spliced" into the film. It is on these spliced images that I will focus now. At four key points in the film before we "meet" Tyler Durden, single images of him are spliced into scenes to flash on screen very quickly. For the purposes of this essay I focus only on the second and third. The second of these occurrences happens six minutes and eighteen seconds into the film as the NP is at the hospital trying to get drugs to help his insomnia. He pleads with the doctor saying that he is in real pain. The doctor responds, "You want to see pain, swing by 1st Methodist Tuesday nights. See the guys with testicular cancer, that's pain" (Fight Club 6:18). At this moment an image of Tyler flashes beside him (that the nameless protagonist does not recognize). Shortly after this the nameless protagonist attends his first support group meeting, "Remaining Men Together". The scene opens with Thomas, one of the group members, relating a personal story. Following this story the group coordinator says, "So let's all of us follow Thomas' example and really open up..." (Fight Club 7:33). It is at this point that the third flash occurs. In this flash Tyler is standing with his arm around the shoulder of the support group coordinator. The call to open up - to be honest - is what elicits this flash (which we are to understand from the camera angle to be the nameless protagonist's point of view). It is demonstrative of his doing exactly the opposite. These flashes indicate his movement away from actuality to spending more and more time "asleep," or rather as his alter ego Tyler Durden. This further underscores the tension between Eliot/Hardy, the privileging of the imaginary/the inability of the imagination to change.

Next I will look at the scene in which the nameless protagonist/Tyler get onto a city bus and see an advertisement for Gucci. The advertisement portrays two men, one facing the audience in tight fitting underwear and the naked facing away where to focus is on his naked bottom. Both men in the advertisement are rather thin. The Edward Norton character turns to Tyler and says "Is that what a man is supposed to look like?" This opposition of the accepted stereotypical norms of male beauty toward the close of the twentieth-century could be said to take up the positivist call to jettison stereotypes and attempt to deal with life as it unfolds. To deal only with the actuality of the world with which we are confronted.

The final scene that I focus on is the scene that both opens and closes the film. Henry Giroux writes,

[w]hile Jack renounces Tyler's militia-like terrorism at the end of F/C, it appears as a meaningless gesture of resistance, as all he can do is stand by and watch as various buildings explode around him. The message here is entirely consistent with the cynical politics that inform the film - violence is the ultimate language, referent, and there is no way of stopping it[10]

Again in focusing only on violence and politics, Giroux misses both the philosophy that informs the film and the film as a philosophy. Let us set the scene and take a closer look. In this scene the nameless protagonist and Tyler are in one of the high-rise buildings with "front row seats for this theatre of mass destruction". Tyler is holding a gun while the nameless protagonist is

---

[10] Giroux (2000), p. 37.

seemingly incapacitated on a rolling desk chair. As Tyler is counting down to when the buildings will be blown up we hear,

NP: You're a fucking hallucination, why can't I get rid of you?"
TD: You need me.
NP: No. I don't. I really don't anymore.
TD: Hey, you created me. I didn't create some loser alter ego to make myself feel better. Take some responsibility (2:10:52-2:11:08).

At this point there is no question that the nameless protagonist and his alter ego are "psychologically and morally at odds," with each other. This precipitates the nameless protagonist's taking control of the situation, realizing that the gun is actually in his hands and shooting himself in the face/mouth, to "kill" Tyler. Although this is perhaps the least believable part of the film the symbolic work it is intended to do is clear. The nameless protagonist has taken over all of his personality again by "killing" Tyler.

At the very end of this final scene the nameless protagonist and Marla occupy the centre of the frame, and while the buildings are collapsing and the Pixies song begins to play, the camera zooms in on his taking Marla's hand, they turn slightly to look at each other, and the Pixies song lyrics come in. The focus of the scene, in terms of what is visually presented on the screen, and the sound (the Pixies song) clearly indicates that violence is not meant to be understood as the ultimate language (the focus is not on the buildings being destroyed in the distance) nor referent. This final scene again demonstrates that it is not only in the absence of women that men are able to create their true identities. In this case what we are visually presented with not only calls into question Giroux's claims, but outright challenges them. Instead of this amounting to a meaningless gesture of resistance, what we see on the screen could be read as pointing in an entirely different direction - that the NP and Marla's coming together is, perhaps, a better answer than a F/C, offering partnership (here with a woman) as what he (we) really need after all. It is no mistake, I think, that when the two take hands they form a heart shape in screen.

From late nineteenth century positivism to the radical realism to late twentieth century Hollywood film, here again Peter Allan Dale is useful,

The end of the nineteenth-century positivist tradition, as [Dale traces] it in the later Darwin, Hardy, and in Freud, is obviously a good way from the beginning of the modernist/postmodernist movement.... It became, rather, the *occasion* for the rise to prominence of a thoroughgoing philosophical aestheticism [one that we find an offshoot of in F/C]. To vary Vaihinger's formula with which [Dale begins], the growth of scientific recognition of 'the impossibility of life' as we would like to believe in it compelled philosophy towards a new and increasingly

unqualified privileging of the imaginary. Humanity followed, as Arnold would
have put it, its ineradicable 'instinct of self-preservation[11]

We find this "unqualified privileging of the imaginary" taken to a new level
in late twentieth-century film, especially films like American Beauty, The
Talented Mr. Ripley, and Fight Club (all released in 1999). The imaginary
evidenced in these films is privileged to such an extent that it both supersedes
and supplants the need or requirement to be grounded to a specific physically
verifiable reality. Once this break with, or departure from, the criterion of
verification occurs, the model of identity construction offered by film allows the
individual to refashion their identity in a manner previously unavailable. It
seems that, within the philosophical framework both offered and supported by
film, these imaginary constructions do provide the energy to change what nature
has given us. Within the logic of the film, however, this framework cannot
support the illusion that it creates, and the change that is affected is at best
ambivalent.

---

[11] Dale (1989), p. 284.

References

Adorno, Theodore (1997). *Aesthetic Theory*. Minneapolis: University of Minnesota Press.
—. (1978). *Minima Moralia: reflections from a damaged life*. Trans. E. F. N. Jephcott. London: Verso.
Dale, Peter Allan (1989). *In Pursuit of A Scientific Culture: Science, Art, and Society in the Victorian Age*. Madison: The University of Wisconsin Press.
Foucault, Michael (1980). *Power/Knowledge*. Ed. Colin Gordon. Trans. Colin Gordon, Leo Marshall, John Mepham, and Kate Soper New York: Pantheon Books.
Freud, Sigmund (1961a). *Five Lectures on Psycho-Analysis*. Trans. James Strachey. NY: W.W. Norton & Company.
—. (1961b) *Civilization and Its Discontents*. Trans. James Strachey. NY: W.W. Norton & Company.
Friday, Krister (2003). `A Generation of Men Without History': Fight Club, Masculinity, and the Historical Symptom. *Postmodern Culture, 13:3*.
Giroux, Henry (2000). Brutalised Bodies and Emasculated Politics: Fight Club, Consumerism, and Masculine Violence. *Border II, Winter 2000-01: 31-41*.

Films

American Beauty, Sam Mendes, 1999, USA
Fight Club, David Fincher, 1999, USA
The Talented Mr. Ripley, Anthony Minghella, 1999, USA
Taxi Driver, Martin Scorsese, 1976, USA

CHAPTER TWO

CITING HEIDEGGER IN *THE THIN RED LINE*

JOLYNNA SINANAN

The Thin Red Line is ostensibly a war film, yet director Terrence Malick defies many of the conventions the audience would expect from a movie about World War II. The 164 minute film depicts a fairly straight forward combat film story: the men of Company C attempt to recapture a hill in Guadalcanal, Solomon Islands from the Japanese. As they confront an unseen enemy, they also confront conflict within themselves. This brief summary is fairly subsidiary to the experience of watching the film, as Malick explores far more than a historical account with fictional characters. At once, Malick's film presents strong references to questions posed by philosopher Martin Heidegger and as a major idea, I will be exploring the appearance of his philosophy which resonates most clearly in the film.

It is interesting to note that Malick was not initially inclined towards cinema in that he did not turn to film making from early in his working life; he was by profession an academic. Malick attended Harvard and majored in philosophy under the guidance of American philosopher Stanley Cavell, subsequently winning a Rhodes scholarship to study in Oxford where he met, worked with and translated a short text by Martin Heidegger. Upon returning to the United States, Malick took up a position as a philosophy lecturer in studies in Heidegger. Consequently, it becomes evident that Malick's deep relationship with philosophy, particularly the works of Heidegger and Cavell's theory of "film as philosophy" has heavily punctuated his meditative war film.

Essentially, Malick's interpretation in *The Thin Red Line* is an exploration of Heidegger's notion of "being" and I will attempt to define and clarify Heidegger's use of the word as it appears in the film. Malick's interest is not in "how the world is", or what facts happen to be true about the world, but, as Hwanhee Lee asserts, in "that it is", "the tragic, uncanny, wondrous and humbling fact of its very existence".[12] The very fact of existence and its

---

[12] Lee (2002).

distinction from nothingness is a prominent line of thought in Heidegger's work, and Malick applies this concern to "war"- the paradox of his understanding the phenomenon of its very existence within this world and within humanity. Because of this cause, Malick is by no means attempting to argue the nature or morality of war, nor does he argue a particular side of the "right" and "wrong" of it, although *The Thin Red Line* is predominantly an anti-war film. Furthermore, Malick contextualises his film within the cinematic history of war films, or more specifically, how World War II and the Vietnam War were portrayed. Although *The Thin Red Line* is a film about World War II, it is more similar in appearance to films of Vietnam, as a reflection of the war film genre.

Thomas Doherty suggests "World War II films painted a portrait of victory and competence of American true grit overcoming stormtrooper discipline and samurai fanaticism. Vietnam erased that image".[13] In Vietnam, there was no distinct evil of "them" against the righteousness of "us", the enemy of the U.S. soldiers was far more complex to confront, understand and overcome - the enemy was within themselves, as seen in post- Vietnam films such as *Apocalypse Now* and *Platoon*.

Also, the enemy was a recognisable figure in the World War II film. While the Allies were fighting the Axis powers, there was a distinct difference between the forces of the axis on screen, Germans were portrayed as inhuman, but the Japanese were portrayed with profuse embitterment; they were subhuman. This particular view is unparalleled in movie history, because as Bernard Dick argues, "Hollywood's revilement of the Japanese was due to the unprovoked and dastardly attack on Pearl Harbour".[14] The "Jap" was certainly not human; he was a lethal, programmed object. For this, the Japanese forfeited the right to individuation; they were "them as the other" in the collective sense. So, on the part of the U.S., as Gilbert Adair suggests, "World War II had been a 'just' war and a necessary one; this war was a crusade. Indeed it was ghastly, but it was inevitable".[15] Less than twenty years later, the ideals that preserved a nation in wartime were shattered, and it is from the viewpoint beyond the next era of war that The Thin Red Line is given .

Most obviously, the Vietnam War film contradicted its predecessor in that it found no larger purpose of war. The unity of the combat squad was ripped open to confront the enemy within amongst the bigger enemy environment. For this, Malick explores underlying themes which are essentially Heideggerian, the common bond between soldiers - they exist within conflict and the immediate threat of death.

---

[13] Doherty (1993), p. 282.
[14] Dick (1985), p. 230.
[15] Adair (1981), p. 132.

Firstly, Malick engages with more of a sense of racial reality, brutality is a factor in war that is fought by teenage boys or young men at least and Malick's representation of the enemy gives them a face, a voice and a conscience. The protagonist, and most prominent character, Witt, comes across the face of a dead Japanese soldier buried in mud, staring up at him and we hear a voice, presumed to be imagined, questioning him, "Are you righteous? Kind?... Are you loved by all? Know that I was too. Do you imagine your sufferings will be less because you loved goodness? Truth?" The voiceover of the protagonist extends from enemy to enemy, he reminds Witt that he is just like him. Malick's attempt to place enemy soldiers on the same level signifies a formidable departure from the World War II film, in which "the Japanese enemy were seldom given an identifiable face, proper name or reaction shot".[16] Similarly, the role of the protagonist in Malick's film is no longer a paternal figure holding the group together; he is more recognisable as the conflicted, lone, existential character from the Vietnam film.

In *The Thin Red Line*, the war Malick explores is internal, his soldiers are in conflict metaphysically and metaphorically as well as physically. In presenting a meditative vision of battle, it becomes apparent that Malick's interest is philosophical and Furstenau and MacAvoy suggest that "Malick puts identifiable philosophical themes in play in the film and raises fundamental questions about the cinema"- or specifically, how Malick uses cinema as an art form that is able to visually convey philosophical notions.[17] American philosopher Stanley Cavell attempts to examine philosophical exploration in film and draws upon the films of Malick. In the introduction to his reflection on film and art, *The World Viewed*, Cavell discusses Malick's *Days of Heaven* and the way Malick frames humans. In short, Malick photographs objects in a reflexive way; the photographic medium is an object which captures, and therefore, objects "participate in the re-creation of themselves on film".[18] So, in turn, humans are dwarfed by the world Malick views; they are apart from it, suggesting that we can never fully capture "ourselves".[19] I will now discuss the basic ideas of the dilemma of Malick's separation of man from the world, the question of man's being or existence, focussing on Heidegger's notions of "being", "authenticity" and "being towards death". Furthermore, I will argue that Malick has deliberately presented an alternative vision of the war film, he

---

[16] Doherty (1993), p 137.
[17] Furstenau, Marc and MacAvoy, Leslie quoted in Patterson (2003), p 174.
[18] Cavell (1971), p. xvi.
[19] For more on Stanley Cavell and representation, see Catherine Wheatley's Chapter Seven: *The Spectator as Moral Agent: Kantian Ethics and the Films of Michael Haneke*, in this book.

engages with his source poetically, rather than re-representing the narrative of the events of battle in the Pacific War. Indeed, Malick has concentrated on making key themes of Heidegger visible, particularly the notion of "being".[20]

Heidegger's *Being and Time* endeavours to clarify the question, "what does it mean to be?" he does not attempt to answer it. Heidegger's primary interest is with ontology, however, he demands that in order to ask the question, one must understand what he is asking, and therefore, Heidegger's idea of being demands that ontology must start from the widest and deepest of distinctions; "the difference between something and nothing". For this, Heidegger creates a system of names in *Being and Time* in order to clarify his objects of discussion as opposed to their use in everyday language. Firstly, Heidegger does not refer to people as "people", or "human beings", he names people, or a person- the fundamental entity that is confronted by an ontological question by the most ordinary of German words to describe exactly what it is: "Dasein", which means "there being". For Heidegger, Dasein is the most unique of creatures, firstly, he can choose the life he leads, he does not merely go through the motions of survival by ingrained instinct and secondly, he is able to manifest individuality by the way he chooses to carry on living. Most importantly, Dasein exists and has the capacity to understand that he exists. In *Being and Time*, Heidegger asserts that "Da-sein is a being that does not simply occur among other beings. Rather he is ontically distinguished by the fact that in his being, this being is concerned about his very being".[21] (Malick explicitly explores the concern of Dasein with the character of Witt, which will be discussed shortly) Also, Dasein is able to comprehend the fact that he will die, one day he will cease to exist. So, the dilemma that Dasein confronts everyday of his life is his relationship with death, or the inevitability that one day he will cease to be. Today he is something, but one day, he will be nothing. In this way, Dasein is also something more; he is always a "being towards death" and the way he relates to the world and to himself with this knowledge will determine how he lives his life - with authenticity or without. With the notion of Dasein, Heidegger's purpose is to convince us that the "essence of man is to understand his being as the possibility that is singly and uniquely his own and nobody else's".[22] The most obvious manifestation of Malick's understanding of Heidegger's notion of being is Private Witt, who opens the film with an ontological question; he meditates on his immediate environment with "What is this war in the heart of nature?" While Malick explores this question binding the threads of war, nature and Heidegger's philosophy in *The Thin Red Line*, it is Witt who launches Malick's investigation and carries the over-seeing perspective of the film.

---

[20] *Ibid*, p. 175.
[21] Mulhall (1996), p. 10.
[22] King (1964), p. 53.

It is Witt's voice we hear at the beginning and end of the film, in his life and death. He witnesses death the most intimately, he touches it and hears it, we are introduced to him with the memory of his dying mother, he attempts to comfort his fellow soldiers when they draw their last breath, and it is his journey to discover how to meet death with "a sense of calm," the manner in which his mother dies. For the most part, we see Guadalcanal through Witt's eyes. He constantly questions the forces around him, even as Charlie Company defeats the Japanese camp, "Where did this great evil come from?... Who's doin' this? Who's killin' us?" And although the sequence depicts victory, it is the extraordinary sense of tragedy that overwhelms the scene as Witt questions the evil that they, the righteous victors harbour. We are reminded of the earlier battle of Staros' regiment, hopelessly ascending the hill, that they are all men who "share one big soul". The enemy soldiers are just as young and afraid of death as the protagonists. Furthermore, it is Witt's questioning of his existence in the war that provides his narrative, he meets his death with a sense of calm and purpose, it is not as Sergeant Welsh warns him, "If you die, it's gonna be for nothing". Witt's death has meaning, he creates a decoy for the company, ultimately sacrificing himself and steering the enemy away from his companions. As well as reflecting Heidegger's notion of being, his death reflects Heidegger's notion of authenticity in the face of the "they", an idea that is exemplified in the conflicting ranks and responsibilities of the soldiers.

The use of military relationships is highly suggestive of Heidegger's notion of the "they", or, most simply as Ree explains, the idea that within the world "we do not fully own ourselves, we are constantly looking over our shoulders and comparing our 'selves' with those of others".[23] The "they" is how we differentiate ourselves (or don't differentiate ourselves) from others, they are the people we speak of when we are concerned with "what people think," not one person in particular, but the people in general, what Heidegger calls "das Man". In living amongst other "Daseins", Dasein tends to lose himself in the "they", Heidegger concedes in *Being and Time* that "The Self of everyday Da-sein is the they-self" and it is "Da-sein's task not to find himself, but to recover what he has originally lost, a sense of himself".[24] To overcome his obscurity within the "they", Dasein must live with authenticity, he must not reject his roles but relate to them authentically; that is with a sense of self and genuine self-understanding. Heidegger describes overcoming inauthenticity as an achievement, as Dasein has regained himself and has not remained lost. Stephen Mulhall explains that

---

[23] Ree (1999), p. 22.
[24] Mulhall (1996), p. 74.

the average, everyday state of Dasein is fundamentally inauthentic, Dasein relates to its work by forgetting itself, entirely subordinating its individuality to the impersonal requirements of the task.[25]

So, by focussing on the model of the combat unit, Malick alludes to the military as the 'they' with its established institution of rank, discipline, language and accolades and furthermore, to the dilemma of Dasein's requirement to act inauthentically with the relationship between Staros and Tall.

When General Quintard approaches Colonel Tall on the bridge of the boat bound for Guadalcanal, Tall is lost in his thoughts of his desire to gain what he feels is owed to him, what he has been waiting for; the years and sacrifices he has given to the military in service will finally result in the victory he deserves. Quintard reminds him that there is "always someone watching, like a hawk," successes and failures will always be noted. Quintard attempt to make conversation with Tall who responds in accordance to a man speaking with a senior officer, with a series of "Yes, sir" and reassures him that he will do and think what is required of him in this position. This sequence contrasts strongly with the first attempt to capture the bunker, in which Sergeant Staros refuses Tall's order to "attack with all the men at his disposal," as Staros is convinced the advance would be a futile suicide mission. Amongst the audience of his juniors, Staros defies his superior on the grounds that he will not send his men to their imminent death. He later tells the men, "You are my sons. You live inside me now. I'll carry you wherever I go". In contrast, when Captain Gaff leads a party of seven to the ridge and captures the bunker, Tall congratulates him and compares him to his son - a salesman. Tall momentarily appears disappointed at the memory of his own past and then regains himself and praises Gaff with the only language he knows, "I'll recommend you for the Silver Star for this, I'll see that you get all you deserve". Tall's comprehension of the attributes of a man consists of Silver Stars and Purple Hearts, the symbols of honour that Staros denies, he chooses the lives of the young men with whom he has lived, rather than the praise of his anonymous peers. Within the ranks of the army, the men are expected to comply to the requirements of their roles, Malick portrays the dilemma of existing authentically as Dasein by exploring the military hierarchy, however, he does not suggest that defying one's orders is necessarily acting with authenticity, it is quite the opposite, it is acting according to one's conscience.

At the beginning of the film, Witt is absent without leave and Malick's deliberate creation of a Melanesian paradise and its contrast to the battle also suggests Witt's inauthenticity and his need to gain a sense of himself within his role as a soldier.

---

[25] *Ibid*, p. 155.

Witt's departure from his company to live amongst the natives signifies his own denial of the world in which he exists. While he is convinced that he "has seen another world," it is the denial of the world in which he bears responsibility that has lead him towards its discovery. In Heidegger's terms, escape is also a form of inauthenticity, it is not ignorant unawareness of one's place, but a deliberate denial of one's place to become swept up in the new, different and unfamiliar. Mulhall explains escape merely as another manifestation of "Dasein's tendency to absorb himself in the 'they'".[26] It is his very role as a soldier that fills Witt with a sense of anxiety in the context of Heidegger. While fear is a conscious sense of dread of something that is known, anxiety is the general existence of dread, or in Witt's case, the knowledge that his role as a soldier may require him to die; for a cause either known, or unknown. Witt begins the path that will lead him to confront his fear of dying, and therefore live authentically by accepting his position in C-Company; by accepting that death is an imminent element in battle, Witt becomes aware of his "being towards death".

As mentioned earlier, the differentiation that marks Heidegger's investigation is between something and nothing, existing or not existing. Ree's interpretation of this notion is that "with its death, Dasein has fulfilled its course".[27] Indeed, Dasein will die and it is with the full acknowledgement that his time in the world will end, fulfilled, or unfulfilled; can Dasein exist in his day to day life authentically. In battle, soldiers are forced to wait to live or die, one can cease to exist at any moment, which reflects Ree's assertion that "in authenticity, each moment is magnified by its possibility of finitude".[28] In the climax of The Thin Red Line, Witt discovers his sense of calm as he leads the enemy troops away from C-Company and finds himself surrounded in an open field. It is interesting to note that throughout the film, we never see Witt fire a single shot and he refuses to now. Even when pursued, Witt does not fire his gun, as if he cannot commit to using his weapon as required of his role, and therefore he is not authentically being a soldier. However, now, he accepts what will happen to him and raises his firearm as expected by the enemy, which we see in a low angle shot. Witt's finitude is marked by ceremony, his funeral and headstone marked by his rifle and his hat. As Sergeant Welsh weeps, it is apparent that although Witt's young life is indeed severed by battle, there is a sense of completeness to his death, he achieves his desired sense of calm and he prolongs the lives of his young companions, at least for one more day. The sense of irony that pervades the sequence as well as the next one is that we are now focussed on Welsh, who witnesses the replacement of Captain Staros and

---

[26] Mulhall (1996), p. 107.
[27] Ree (1999), p 37.
[28] *Ibid*, p. 43.

laments the pointlessness of their presence, yet it is Tall who is actually correct in his assumptions; Guadalcanal was the military turning point in the Pacific War, and their experience is tragic, yet necessary to the end of the war. At this point, Malick seems to suggest that one must live inauthentically in order to survive, and it is the dilemma between living and surviving that his characters are grappling with, hence the overwhelming sense of nature. In nature, it is the battle for survival that maintains the balance between living creatures; and regarding conflict in nature, it appears that the same principle applies. By locating war in the prominent foreground of nature, Malick reduces beings to the most animalistic level - they struggle to survive and forgo the unique capacity to live their lives.

Although this overview of Heidegger's philosophy has been simplified and condensed, it provides the underlying philosophical themes of Malick's film. *The Thin Red Line* ends with a close up shot of the water's surface, broken in a repetitive motion by the departing boat. It is only with the previous long shot we realise it is C-Company leaving. They have accomplished their mission, however, there is no sense of real closure or finality as the shot fades out, as Witt's voice poses the question , "Darkness and light, strife and love - are they the workings of one mind, the features of the same face?" and concludes with, "Oh my soul... let me be in you now. Look out through my eyes, look out at the things you made, all things shining". Malick has reached no resolution to his question, "What is this war in the heart of nature," yet he has pointed his audience in the direction of discovering the meaning of the question from which to ask further questions. If *The Thin Red Line* is indeed an example of Heidegger's ideas in a cinematic form, it ends in the same way *Being and Time* unfolds, as Ree explains,

> if we end up discovering nothing positive, we can at least hope to clarify our understanding of the question we are asking, the 'question of the meaning of being.[29]

Through a sophisticated use of visual, literary and cultural poetics, Malick explores the fundamental meaning of the concepts of "war" and "nature" as we understand them. Furtenau and MacAvoy describe war as "a distinctly human phenomenon, despite its inhumanity".[30] Drawing upon Heidegger's notion of "being towards death"- that every being is essentially thrown towards death by the indifference of nature and time, it is only a human being who can will death upon himself, another or others on a massive scale. This explicit point appears to embody Malick's fascination with the nature of war, that in the existing world

---

[29] Ree (1999), p. 4.
[30] Furstenau and MacAvoy in Patterson (2003), p 181.

of natural, inherent conflict, there is a darkness that harbours the will to destroy another and Malick explores several facets of this paradox in his protagonists who are essentially by character "all faces of the same man". The common uniting force is expressed visually by the soldiers' uniforms, that when they are given their orders by Tall, he is filmed in the background, surrounded by a sea of indistinguishable khaki hard hats. Malick's unique take of the war film presents a far more important point for consideration than merely establishing who is "good" and "bad" in war and why; he suggests that the force for violence exists and the destruction it causes is regrettable by all parties. War is a force that needs to be explained, it is not an occurrence and it is not in itself a consequence of political and cultural dilemmas. However, Malick does not proceed to "explain" the force of war, nor does he demonstrate its instance. Malick treats war in the same manner he cinematically treats nature. War is larger and is more destructive than man, yet it is not a distant force like nature, it is born from the same place as our compassion and love - it spawns from our very being. The internal aspect of conflict is what perplexes Malick most of all and what he encourages the audience to reflect upon. The most powerful aspect of conflict as presented by Malick is that the tragedy of the fear, suffering and killing is so overwhelmingly personal, that, as Ron Mottram describes,

> it feeds into the larger philosophical and moral issues of the film; that which pits human beings against each other as enemies.[31]

In this way, *The Thin Red Line* is possibly the most profound war movie of the post World War II era.

---

[31] Mottram, Ron, quoted in Patterson (2003), p. 20.

Acknowledgements

Thank you to Dr Roger Hillman and Dr Graham Jones for their invaluable discussion in developing this chapter.

References

Adair, Gilbert (1981). *Hollywood's Vietnam Film: From 'The Green Berets' to 'Apocalypse Now'*. New York: Proteus Publication Company.
Cavell, Stanley (1971). *The World Viewed: Reflections on the Ontology of Film*. Cambridge: Harvard University Press.
Dick, Bernard F. (1985). *The Star-Spangled Screen: The American World War II Film*. Lexington: The University Press of Kentucky.
Doherty, Thomas (1993). *Projections of War, Hollywood, American Culture and World War II*. New York: Columbia University Press.
King, Magda (1964). *Heidegger's Philosophy: A Guide to His Basic Thought*. New York: The Macmillian Company.
Lee, Hwanhee (2002). 'Great Directors- A Critical Database: Terrence Malick,' *Senses of Cinema*, [on-line] http://www.sensesofcinema.com/ contents/directors/02/malick.html [accessed 15/07/2003].
Morrison, James and Schur, Thomas (2003). *The Films of Terrence Malick*. Westport: Praeger Publishers.
Mulhall, Stephen (1996). *Heidegger and 'Being and Time'*. London, Routledge.
Patterson, Hannah (ed.) (2003). *The Cinema of Terrence Malick: Poetic Visions of America*. London: Wallflower.
Ree, Jonathan (1999). *Heidegger*. London: Routledge.

Films

Apocalypse Now, Francis Ford Coppola, 1979, USA
Days of Heaven, Terrence Malick, 1978, USA
Platoon, Oliver Stone, 1986, USA
The Thin Red Line, Terrence Malick, 1998, USA

CHAPTER THREE

THE CINEMATIC CLOSE-UP: REFLECTIONS IN LIGHT OF THE PHILOSOPHY OF EMMANUEL LEVINAS

ORNA RAVIV

In this paper, I will discuss the interface between cinematic theory and the philosophy of Emmanuel Levinas. I am especially interested in discussing the manner in which Levinas' concept of the face can illuminate the discussion of the close-up, and the manner in which the notion of close-up can clarify the concept of the face.

According to Levinas, the face has a transcendental status, and constitutes a key concept in his ethics. His metaphysical theory is unique in the history of philosophy in that it grants ethics a primary place. Levinas is opposed to the manner in which Western philosophy assimilates the concept of knowledge as a regulative ideal. According to Levinas, knowledge and accordingly, the concept of the intentional object, are the basis of a human relationship to the world that does not allow the Other to appear.

The Other is a central concept in Levinas' philosophy. It is a concept that relates to the dimension of the unknown in the person that one is facing. This dimension is unrecognizable and incomprehensible. Levinas states:

> The absolutely other is the Other... Neither possession nor unity of number nor the unity of concepts link me to the Stranger...Over him I have no power. He escapes my grasp by an essential dimension...[32]

According to Levinas, this transcendent dimension disappears completely in our ordinary ways of encountering the person in front of us. The Other cannot appear because knowledge and understanding underlies our basic position towards the real world. The human subject, who is controlled by the need to

---

[32] Levinas (1969), p. 39.

know, recognizes and understands the person standing before her by making that person similar to herself.

To know amounts to grasping being out of nothing or reducing it to nothing, removing from it its alterity.[33]

According to Levinas, understanding is the conversion of the external object of thought into something identical to the thought in our mind. In other words, the subject completely assimilates the object, and conceals its radical externalism.

The idea that the subject converts the external object into a mental representation is the notion of intentionality so central in Western philosophy. Intentionality is the link between our conscious states, such as thinking, desires, dreams, passions on the one hand, and the objects to which they are directed. Correlatively, the objects in the world appear to us as mental representations. This process is extremely creative. In essence, representation ascribes a meaning to the object that does not really belong to it. In this process, the object's otherness disappears. What remains is only the manner in which it is represented in the subject's consciousness. The differentiation between the object of representation and the subject and between the inside and the outside world is eliminated, and the object becomes a part of the subject's consciousness:

> In clarity the exterior being presents itself as the work of the thought that receives it. Intelligibility, characterized by clarity, is a total adequation of the thinker with what is thought, in the precise sense of a mastery exercised by the thinker upon what is thought in which the object's resistance as an exterior being vanished [34]

Levinas claims that understanding is identical to representing. Since understanding erases the identity of the person in front of the subject, and all that remains is its representation, the desire for knowledge, together with thinking about consciousness as intentional, therefore do not allow the Other to appear.

Levinas proposes an alternative – an analysis of the human face as the place in which the Other appears, and in which ethics are expressed. For him, our encounter with the human face can not be understood in terms of relationship between subject and object.

Levinas claims that the face is not only a combination of nose, forehead, eyes, etc, that together constitute a particular enclosed object. The face is different from any familiar object because it is difficult to define exactly where the face begins and where it ends. Its boundaries are both defined and

---

[33] *Ibid*, p. 44.
[34]*Ibid*. p. 124.

undefined. On the one hand, the face presents itself in a clear, identifiable and understandable manner; while on the other hand, it opens a new dimension that exposes the depth of existence. The face can present itself but it cannot be represented

Therefore, the face cannot be defined in terms of its internal or external features. The face cannot be defined as an object and it is not possible to differentiate between its form and content. A coin has two opposite sides. After one side is viewed, it can be turned over so that the reverse side is visible and the other side is no longer visible. The face, on the other hand, does not constitute the external side of anything. It is not like a façade of a building that hides the interior. The face represents the place in which the internal and external are blended together.[35]

The face is therefore not an object. It cannot be concisely defined by observation, and it is not perceived by processes of representation. Levinas states that the face represents more than what it is. For this reason, the face cannot be completely understood. The face of the person in front of me does not allow itself to be an object that can be seen or touched by me.

> The relation with the face is not an object-cognition. The transcendence of the face is at the same time its absence from this world into which it enters, the exiling of a being, his condition of being stranger...[36]

Facing a face I cannot recognize or understand it. I cannot make it part of my cognition. Thus, the face is not subject to control or recognition by the observer and remains eternally unknown. Openness to this dimension of the face is in effect openness to the Other.

The Other appears in the face. But if the face of the Other is not an object, if it does not allow itself to be seen or understood, what does the concept of the face mean?

Despite the fact that the concept of the face is central to Levinas' discourse, he refrains from providing concrete examples of it. Does he mean its visual dimension? Is the face a metaphor? What kind of relationships can be created in a face-to-face encounter? Can such relationships exist in familiar everyday reality?

I would like to argue that cinema provides a concrete face-to-face encounter in which otherness can show itself without being objectified. In particular I think that the cinematic close-up can serve as a fruitful framework in which Levinas' concept of the face can be clarified. I shall turn now to a brief analysis

---

[35] *Ibid*, p. 197.
[36] *Ibid*, p. 75.

of the close-up through which I hope that Levinas' concept of the face to be understood in a more concrete fashion.

The close-up is a photograph of the face from very close proximity. The use of the close-up began as a gimmick, that is, to achieve a stylistic effect, but theoretical discussion of the close-up developed to the point that the close-up is now viewed as a special cinematic phenomenon. In view of the special status of the notion of the close-up in cinema, I would like to consider whether it could be used to elucidate Levinas' concept of the face.

The close-up was first used in 1901 by George Meliès. It was called "the large head", since it was mainly used to enlarge the face of the protagonists. The meaning of the term "close-up" is perhaps connected to the fact that Meliès's close-up was not an image of the actor's face chosen from a space that contained other surrounding objects, but rather a face isolated by a circle, and the area surrounding it was black or white. In other words, the face was enclosed and brought forward in "close-up". Meliès's close-ups appeared suddenly throughout the movie, and therefore created an element of surprise and novelty. A good example for this use of the close-up is in *The Great Train Robbery* (1903) a film by Edvin F. Porter.[37] At the end of this short film that tells the story of a train robbed by a gang, there is a close-up of one of the robbers. He takes a gun and shoots in the direction of the camera. This close-up has nothing to do with the story of the film and serves only to achieve a stylistic effect.

The close-up was later used as a means of showing things that could not be seen from far away, such as actors' facial expressions. In the early films, the camera was always placed at a distance in a position relative to the viewer's position in the theatre (what is called a "long shot").The idea that the camera could be moved hadn't yet been suggested by anyone. Actors were therefore forced to exaggerate their facial expression as they would in the theatre. In order to allow their facial expressions to be visible, the camera lens was moved closer while the camera remained in place. During the shot itself, the actors had to repeat exactly the same facial expressions that had been photographed from far away in order to provide a more detailed view. In this way, the close-up was no more than a way of showing viewers what they had already seen, while emphasizing details that they might have missed.[38]

The first person to move a camera from the long shot position was D. W. Griffith. Griffith was the first to move the camera closer to an actor to a position known as the "full shot". After the full-shot position, the next logical step was to move the camera even closer to the position known as the close-up. Griffith's creation of the close-up was a continuation of his great innovation. This step

---

[37] This close-up is considered to be the first close-up in cinema (as an image separated from the surroundings).
[38] Eisenstein (1982), p 242.

aroused strong opposition among critics, who claimed that to simply show heads is against the rules of filmmaking.[39]

Griffith used the close-up in a way that complemented the long shot and the full shot, and in so doing, transformed the use of the close-up from a casual gimmick into a dramatic element. His main use of the close-up was to create atmosphere, to show his heroes' personality traits or moods, or to symbolize meaning. Close-ups of objects symbolized inner conflicts or thoughts, or offered psychological interpretations of the characters' behaviour. In this context, Griffith's use of the close-up was symbolic. Shooting objects from close proximity was intended to create an atmosphere that would reveal the characters' inner world, symbolizing a particular mood. For example, in the film *Avenging Conscience* (1914) by Griffith, in one of the scenes in a court, while a witness is testifying, Griffith uses a close-up of his hand anxiously grabbing a handkerchief in order to show how nervous the witness is.

At the same time Griffith also used close-ups of faces. His use of the face, however, was not significantly different from that of objects. Griffith used close-ups of his characters' faces mainly to enhance dialogues and to move from one speaking character to another. Another way in which Griffith used close-ups of the characters in the film was to create a particular rhythm in a scene by moving from one shot to another, with the longest time devoted to the long shot, less time devoted to the full shot, and the least time devoted to the close-up.[40] In other words, Griffith's use of the close-up of the face was done in a dramatic context, and designed to do no more than enhance the plot.

Despite the importance of the cinematic novelty of the close-up, Griffith's technique aroused criticism, particularly among Russian formalists, the most prominent of which was Sergei Eisenstein.

Eisenstein claimed that the close-up must "free" the film from the plot, rather than serve it. His claim concerning the close-up is part of his cinematic theory, and cannot be understood without addressing this framework. Eisenstein was looking for a new way in which cinema could express ideas, rather than merely tell a story. His conception is based on the theory of idealism – in other words, the belief that the film must constitute an independent ideational world. According to this approach, the highest form of cinema is intellectual cinema. This form of cinema must be detached from any story, plot, or living person, and must relay ideas – mainly social ideas – using formal language.[41] *The Battleship Potyomkin* (1925) is a film about a workers' rebellion that is cruelly suppressed by the army. Just after the famous scene on the stairway in Odessa where the camera follows a baby trolley falling down the stairs, Eisenstein

---

[39] Bazin (1971), p. 15.
[40] Eisenstein (1957), p. 199.
[41] *Ibid.*, p. 46.

shows three shots of lions photographed next to each other in such a way that the stone statues come to life. His intention is not to tell any particular story, but rather to express the idea of the Russian worker's awakening.

According to Eisenstein, in order to express an idea rather than a story, the connection between the various shots must be an abstract one. The close-up facilitates such an abstract connection. In the other types of shots – the long shot and the full shot, reality is always present, and the connection to the concrete is always apparent. (Reality is present in the images of objects that comprise it; a stove, a cup, a towel, a bench, a tablecloth). Therefore, use of the long shot will always leave the film tied to reality, and the image that appears in it will always be individual and particular. Eisenstein claims that in order to express an idea, it is necessary to free ourselves of the particular in favour of the general.

> Such an abstraction of the lifelike may in certain instances be given by the close-up. A skilfully leading montage creation with close-ups... isolated from naturalism and abstracted in the necessary direction... could well have been lifted...[42]

In a close-up, the details that create the particular are absent, and it therefore does not contain reality. There is only a face on the screen, and this face is completely anonymous. Therefore, the close-up is the only type of shot that facilitates the abstraction from everyday reality.

Eisenstein's discussion of the close-up, therefore, demonstrates his general view on the essence of cinema. On the one hand, Eisenstein frees the close-up from the level of representation and symbolism. On the other hand, he uses the conception of the close-up to argue against realism in cinema.

The theory of realism in cinema is based on the idea that the magnitude and uniqueness of cinema lies in its ability to give us a realistic and complete image of reality. Since the camera is a mechanical device, the images that it presents are objective. The camera, therefore, allows cinema to show things objectively. Cinema is therefore capable of presenting things in a pure manner. One of the theoreticians who represents this realistic approach is Andre Bazin.[43]

Bazin claims that cinema should not use the close-up. Using the close-up means adhering to the viewpoint of the protagonist of the film or its director. It means showing the relationships between the images of reality as perceived by them, and not as they really are.

---

[42] Bazin (1971), p. 15.

The facts follow one another, and the mind is forced to observe their resemblance: and thus, by recalling one another, they end by meaning something which was inherent in each...[44]

Bazin's idea is that reality does not need to serve any particular viewpoint. Every detail of reality, every image, existed before our consciousness attributed meaning to it, and this is the manner in which they should appear in a movie.

The films of the Italian Neorealist directors made at the end of the fifties express realistic ideas about the nature of cinema. In *Bicycle Thieves* (1948), a film by Vittorio De Sica, the viewer follows a father and son looking for bicycles that had been stolen from the father. Without the bicycles, the father can't go to work. In one of the scenes, the father suddenly sees someone holding what he believes to be his bicycle. In a classic film, the viewer would expect to first see a close-up of the father followed by a close-up of what he sees, namely the bicycle. Instead, De Sica chooses to show the whole street with people and cars and bicycles without focusing or emphasizing what is important to the protagonist of the film, that is to say, his bicycles.

Realism in cinema therefore attempts to express the manner in which things appear in reality, without ascribing importance to any particular detail or point of view. For this reason, realism will use fewer cinematic techniques that involve choosing an image, separating it from time and space, and granting it an increased measure of importance. This is the reason that realistic cinema deliberately makes little use of the close-up.

The discussion of the close-up in cinema, therefore, touches on issues which have occupied cinema theoreticians, and which are connected to the essence of cinema. They deal with the relations between cinema and reality and the manner in which cinematic means should serve the basic cinematic concepts. This discourse raises claims concerning the connection of the close-up to time and space, the manner in which the close-up symbolizes feelings and mental states, and the way in which it represents the specific point of view and state of affairs.

Another theoretical approach which is particularly relevant to my discussion of the close-up examines the concept of affect.

Affect is the dimension of experience that acts upon feelings, rather than upon our perception. Perception is the manner in which we recognize the world and are aware of the qualities of its objects such as colours, smells, tastes, as well as their shapes and their respective position in relation to each other. We express perception by means of action. We recognize the object in front of us, and act accordingly. On the other hand, the body reacts to the affective, emotional dimension of experience by means of expression. Our feelings and sensations are expressed in our face.

---

[44] *Ibid.*, p. 36.

Since a close-up is a photograph of the face taken in close proximity, it allows the affective dimension to be visible and can therefore be called an affective image.

Jean Epstein was among the first cinema theoreticians who referred to the affective dimension of the close-up. Epstein describes the expression that is created on a face. He claims that the face on the screen expresses a range of feelings. This range of feelings is expressed in the close-up by the way that eyelashes flutter, eyebrows arch, the forehead wrinkles up, the chin moves, and the nostrils close. In other words, according to Epstein, the expression that is created by the face is created by minimal, intensive movements.[45]

On the other hand, Epstein claims that he never understood a close-up in which there was no movement. He claims that close-ups of this type sacrifice the essence of cinema in general, and of the close-up in particular, which is movement. According to Epstein, the close-up constitutes the greatest expression of the photographic quality of movement that the cinema camera can express because of its intensiveness.[46]

Gilles Deleuze disagrees with Epstein's assertion, and claims that intensive movement and lack of movement are two opposite poles that appear in the face, and therefore appear in the close-up as well:

> Rather than an exclusive origin, it is a matter of two poles, sometimes one prevailing over the other and appearing almost pure, sometimes the two being mixed in one direction or the other.[47]

Deleuze refers to these two poles as power and quality, and claims that they express two different mental states. The first state is the one that Epstein refers to in which a facial expression is created as a result of intensive nerve activity. Deleuze calls this a state of Power. This state expresses a wide range of feelings that are connected to passion. An example of a close-up of Power can be seen in *Casablanca* by Michael Curtiz (1942). The film tells the story of two former lovers who meet in Casablanca during World War II. Ingrid Bergman is Ilsa, who arrives to Casablanca with her husband Victor Lazlo. She has no choice but to ask her former lover Rick (Humphrey Bogart) for help. When Rick refuses to help her, a close-up reveals a whole range of expressions in Ingrid's face. The viewer can watch her facial expression change from anger to love, from love to passion, and from passion to compassion.

---

[45] Epstein (1988), p. 239.
[46] *Ibid*, p. 237.
[47] Deleuze (2001), p. 88.

The other state, in which facial expressions are created without movement, is referred to by Deleuze as a state of Quality. In a state of Quality, the protagonist's face is almost still and expresses thought or wonder.

Facial expressions can contain various intensities of these two poles of Quality and Power. In addition, we often see a facial expression change before our very eyes in a single shot – moving from an expression of wonder to another extreme that expresses strong passion or intense anger.

A series of facial expressions of this type can only be seen in a close-up. Epstein states that the close-up allows "microscopic drama", as he calls it, to be seen by the viewer. The reason for this is that the close-up enables the viewer to be closer to the face of the person on the screen than any experience in reality. What is the significance of this proximity? Does it merely enable me to see the details of the face better, or does it have other connotations?

Jean Mitry claims that the close-up creates a sensual impression more than an intellectual one. Film observers experience and feel the image more than they understand it. In other words, in a shot from far away, viewers see objects as they appear in everyday reality, and must understand the relations between them. Close-up plays upon the emotions, and therefore understanding is a minor factor. For this reason, the difference between the close-up and the long shot is not the scale of size or the field of vision. The difference lies in the manner in which the close-up affects the viewer and his sensations and feelings. In this way, the close-up as an affective image does not only express the feelings of the character but also has an impact on the feelings of the observer, as Mitry states:

> Pain is put within reach. If I stretch out my hand, I am in contact with the inner being. I can count the lashes of the suffering. I can taste the salt of its tears. Never before has a face been so close to mine. It follows me even closer and yet it is I who am following it, face to face...[48]

In this sense the close-up acts upon our senses in a way that is different from reality. In the close-up, the proximity to the face enables the viewer to feel what the person standing opposite is feeling, in a manner that everyday reality does not allow. The observer experiences and feels the image and does not need to understand it.

The above discussion of the close-up as a phenomenon involving senses rather than rational understanding brings me back to the beginning of this discussion, that is, to Levinas. Levinas states:

---

[48]Mitry (1997), p. 135.

Rather than taking sensation to be contents to fill a priori form of objectivity, a transcendental function *sui generis* must be recognized in them... The senses have a meaning that is not predetermined as objectification...[49]

According to Levinas, it is through the senses or the affect that objectivity disappears. The senses enable us to meet the world in a different way. The person in front of us is no longer an object of our knowledge and understanding. Levinas claims that the representational content of the senses dissolves into their affective content.

As suggested, Levinas does not really provide any concrete example that could help us understand better his claims. I think that the close-up, once we see it as an affective image can serve as a good example for Levinas' claims about sensuality and objectivity. In looking at the close-up, the viewer experiences the feeling that appears on the face in a way that does not depend upon what causes it. In other words, what we see in the close-up is not fear caused by something, but rather fear itself. When the face of the image expresses fear, the viewer does not need to actually see a knife in order to feel a sense of fear. In this sense when we see the expression of pain in a close-up, we see pain itself, regardless of the object or the state of affairs that caused it.

In this way, the close-up impacts the feelings of the observer, and therefore allows something deep to appear that does not depend on any particular object. As an experience that acts on the senses and not on understanding, the close-up constitutes pure experience which does not depend on objective content. What appears on the screen is primary, unprocessed feeling, devoid of content. The close-up, then, allows the observer to be exposed to the affective dimension of experience in a way that is different from real life or every-day experience.

Hence, I would like to end this discussion with the following questions: What are the repercussions of the close-up as an affective image? Can the close-up serve as a point of view for discussing Levinas' concept of the Other? If so, can Levinas' concept of the face allow us to add additional, ethical content to cinematic discourse in general, and to the discussion of the close-up in particular?

---

[49] Levinas (1969), p. 188.

References

Bazin, André (1971). *What is Cinema*. Berkeley: University of California Press.
Deleuze, Gill (2001). *Cinema 1*. Minneapolis: University of Minnesota Press.
Eisenstein, Sergei (1957). *Film Form*. New York: Meridian Books.
—. (1982). *Film Essays and Lectures*. Edited by Leyda J. New York: Princeton University Press.
Epstein, Jean (1988). Magnification. In Abel Richard (ed), *French film Theory and Criticism, A History/Anthology, 1907-1939, Vol. 1*. Princeton, N.J: Princeton University Press.
Levinas, Emanuel (1969). *Totality and Infinity*. Translated by Alphonso Lingis. Pennsylvania: Duquesne University Press.
Mitry Jean (1997). *The aesthetics and psychology of the cinema*. Bloomington: Indiana University Press.

Films

The Great Train Robbery, Edvin F. Porter, 1903, USA
Avenging Conscience, D. W. Griffith, 1914, USA
The Battleship Potyomkin, Sergei Eisenstein, 1925, Soviet Union
Bicycle Thieves, Vittorio De Sica, 1948, Italy
Casablanca, Michael Curtiz, 1942, USA

CHAPTER FOUR

AGAINST FILMED THEATRE

JOHN ADAMS

> "Cinema, radio, television, magazines are a school of
> inattention: people look without seeing, listen in without
> hearing"
>
> *Robert Bresson*

People are accustomed to watching films in a certain way, encouraged by the filmmakers themselves, who produce noisy, provocative (the desire to make us think), fast moving works, discouraging the viewers from contemplating the images before them. Much of what we see on film *doesn't* encourage us to take the medium seriously. (From Saul Bellow, on *Psycho*: "Nothing but conditioned reflexes they've trained you into [...]. Logical connections are lacking and the gaps are filled with noises-sound effects. You have to give up on coherence. They keep you uneasy and give you one murder after another"[50]) I have, for a long time, held onto certain fundamental ideas concerning film, or the importance of film. I think, for example, that film can be a very great art form, placed within the tradition of established art forms, and that for this to be so there has to be a single mind behind its creation. Why this has to be so will become apparent. I do not argue my case, but attempt elucidation.

Perhaps, of Western film directors, Robert Bresson and Andrei Tarkovsky come closest to this ideal. Certainly Bresson has as much control over his films as a director can have. Those familiar with his work will know that he was almost comically uncompromising, refusing to follow the path of other filmmakers in those aspects most often considered so important in film: acting, camera movement, music, sounds, plot. He is one of those few filmmakers whose consistency, singularity of vision and determination mean that their films can be said to transcend genre or to be their own genre. But more importantly, the methods he used (or didn't use) give his films a contemplative quality. He famously rejected the techniques of cinema (acting, music and so on), instead

---

[50] Bellow (1987), p. 232.

offering pared down works (cinematography), which cannot be compared with mainstream cinema, that say as much as possible with the sparest of means. It seems to me that he was trying to rid the medium of everything contrived, obvious, to leave things as they are, to show things as they are, not to express what we now expect to be expressed in film.

But first a word about Bresson's use of terms. When he talks of cinema he means filmed theatre. True works of cinematography are not photographed theatre. (He writes that there are two types of film: "those that employ the resources of the theatre (actors, direction, etc.) and use the camera in order to *reproduce*; those that employ the resources of cinematography and use the camera to *create*"[51]) These are not populated by actors but by what he calls "models": "An actor in cinematography might as well be in a foreign country. He does not speak its language".[52] So what are considered true or pure films are cinematography and the director is the cinematographer (though the filmmaker doesn't "direct", as we shall see). But we need to clarify his notion of models.

Why did he disapprove so strongly of acting and actors in film? Right from his early years as a filmmaker he saw things clearly: "No actors. (No directing of actors) No parts. (No learning of parts) No staging. But the use of working models, taken from life. BEING (models) instead of SEEMING (actors)".[53] What he means by "being", I think, is that the characters are his creation, true to themselves, as he wants them to be, living in their own world, *appearing* to have their own life. Theatrical techniques have no role here. So what is wrong with the theatre? Nothing is wrong with the theatre. And nothing is wrong with acting. Part of the problem is illustrated in the following statement:

> The photographed theatre or CINEMA requires a *metteur-en-scene* or director to make some actors perform a play and to photograph these actors performing the play; afterwards he lines up the images. Bastard theatre lacking what makes theatre: material presence of living actors, direct action of the audience on the actors.[54]

Actors belong in the theatre. *But what is wrong with actors in a film?* "Nothing rings more false in a film than that natural tone of the theatre copying life and traced over STUDIED SENTIMENTS".[55] Perhaps most importantly: "Movement from exterior to interior. (Actors: movement from interior to exterior)" Actors, good actors, express their feelings (or rather feelings

---

[51] Bresson (1986), p. 5.
[52] *Ibid.*, p. 6.
[53] *Ibid.*, p. 4.
[54] *Ibid.*, p. 7.
[55] *Ibid.*, p. 8.

appropriate to the part) in a certain way and the audience reacts, are stimulated. A certain type of actor might be able to reduce the audience to tears with an emotional performance. With actors who are consciously trying to be other people, not themselves, and their creativity, not only gives the thing a theatrical feel, that is not suited to the medium, but also detracts from the feeling one gets that it is a director's film that is being watched, it breaks up the film. And there is the sense that one is being manipulated, sometimes almost bullied into feelings of heightened emotion.

A superficial reading of Bresson will show this unambiguous view of performance, this distaste for actors, acting parts, taking roles, the actor consciously performing as he might imagine a character to be, the feelings, that he or the director thinks that character has: 'X is imitating Napoleon, whose nature was not to imitate.'[56] But what is important here for the viewer can be illustrated by Bresson's view of models and how they should be trained:

> A model. Enclosed in his mysterious appearance. He has brought home to him all of him that was outside. He is there, behind that forehead, those cheeks […]. Radically suppress *intentions* in your models […]. To your models: 'Don't think what you're saying, don't think what you're doing.' And also: Don't think *about* what you say, don't think *about* what you do […]. Nine-tenths of our movements obey habit and automatism. It is anti nature to subordinate them to will and to thought […]. Models who have become automatic (everything weighed, measured, timed, repeated ten, twenty times) and are then dropped in the medium of the events of your film – their relations with the objects and persons around them will be *right*, because they will not be *thought*.[57]

There is no self-consciousness here, no awareness of non-acting, the models have been reduced to automatons, without thought. It is Bresson, as cinematographer and only him, who knows what the characters in the films should be, the characters themselves and their movements are not related to the narrative until the director puts everything together. The models are fitted into the narrative as he thinks they should be. They are given equal status, in the film, as animals, trees, cars: "Model. Two mobile eyes in a mobile head, itself on a mobile body".[58] They are just one part of the film, a fragment which the cinematographer fits into everything else, each fragment is important, each has a specific part to play in the finished film, as it is in life. Everything is necessary. There is a unity, a balance: "The persons and objects in your film must *walk at the same pace, as companions*".[59] The director, perhaps, is not so much editing

---

[56] *Ibid.*, p. 25.
[57] Ibid., pp. 15-22.
[58] *Ibid.*, p. 29.
[59] *Ibid.*, p. 69.

as selecting moments. (But what must be recognised is that his characters come from him, are part of him: "Make yourself homogeneous with your models, make them homogeneous with you"[60])

The importance of his approach lies here. And this, I think, leads to the deeper, more evocative nature of his films. Instead of an actor expressing his emotion, trying to convey feeling, becoming the focus of our attention, of the film, we are given nothing obvious to respond to. A glance, a single tear drop, a movement of the hand, a lowering of the head all play vital roles. These things are not illustrative. Like the sounds or music he once used ("Silence, musical by an effect of resonance. The last syllable of the last word, or the last noise, like a held note"[61]), or the editing of images, these ordinary movements, gestures, drained of self-consciousness merely point the way, they are an indicator. But to what? The very real mystery, the human soul, human feeling, what lies beneath the surface. Nothing is as explicit as in an actor's film. No explanation. (But what is there to explain anyway?) Human gestures are just human gestures. Yet we see them through our own experiences. Why should there be acting? One sees, when used to this approach (and I do think one has to get used to it, one needs to train oneself to see these films differently), how *meaningful* a glance can be. The extraordinary power of a particular look or utterance. Through the use of ordinary movements, one is directed (that is all) towards a world of feeling. A movement of the hand, of the head, of the eyes, the walk, the placing of one image in a particular point in time can reveal or suggest depths that the simple, ordinary movements and images appear to belie. There is no manipulation here, again we are not told what to think or feel, we are not *told* to think or feel, it is only through contemplating such images that we experience their power ("Do not try, and do not wish, to draw tears from the public with the tears of your models, but with this image rather than that one, this sound rather than that one, exactly in their place"[62]). In the final moments of *Mouchette* a young girl commits suicide. One feels that there is something more to it, a real power, depth. There is nothing gratuitous in Bresson's world, but what are we to make of it? All great art is mysterious, and *Mouchette*'s end is full of it. As the girl rolls down the slope and into the clear water, she disappears from view. But where does she go? Of course this question doesn't arise, cannot arise after what we have been shown (we might ask such a question of a bad film). Here it is the beauty of Monteverdi that evokes another world, where it suggests, evokes the feeling that Mouchette's death might not be meaningless, but nothing more than that. But it is the very lack of expression on the girl's face that is so powerful. Perhaps Bresson means something similar when he writes:

---

[60] *Ibid.*, p. 45.
[61] *Ibid.*, p. 89.
[62] *Ibid.*, p. 128.

CINEMA seeks *immediate* and *definitive* expression through mimicry, gestures, intonations of voice. This system inevitably excludes expression through contacts and exchanges of images and of sounds and the transformations that result from them.[63]

Or more explicitly: "Images, conductors of the gaze. BUT THE ACTOR'S ACTING THROWS THE EYE".[64] Actors acting tell you what to do. There simply isn't room for contemplation, no time. The actor distracts the viewer with his habit (Bresson talks of "the terrible habit of theatre"[65]). But the model's apparently empty gaze, by its very emptiness, is supremely evocative of a world of feeling, absent from most performances. Cinema gives us action and emotions, without doubts, ambivalence. We might be moved by a performance, but that is nothing more than physiological stimulation, an increase in heart rate, without being shown any kind of understanding of the world, of what makes us tick. Another quote:

To put sentiments on his face and into his gestures is the art of the actor, is theatre. Not to put sentiments on his face and into his gestures is (still) not cinematography. Involuntarily expressive models (not wilfully inexpressive ones).[66]

I've always felt that this is a poke at other directors who use actors in a very restrained way, most famously Michelangelo Antonioni. For once more, it should be emphasised that the models are not being restrained, consciously keeping everything inside. They are just living, being themselves outside the context of any narrative, the director can be seen as giving life to these people. But what does he mean by the phrase "involuntarily expressive"? The point is that the models are expressive, but it is, as one critic put it, "the spiritual expressiveness of the blank face":[67] "Models, mechanized externally, internally free. On their faces nothing wilful '*The constant, the eternal beneath the accidental.*'"[68] The passivity, shyness of his characters do appear somewhat robotic, stiff to the unsympathetic eye and curiously out of place in contemporary life, or film. But the director isn't trying to be contemporary. Indeed, from the same critic:

---

[63] *Ibid.*, p. 36.
[64] *Ibid.*, p. 44.
[65] *Ibid.*, p. 6.
[66] *Ibid.*, p. 71.
[67] Thomson (1980), p. 68.
[68] Bresson (1986), p. 46.

It might be said that watching Bresson is to risk conversion from cinema. His meaning is so inspirational, and his treatment so remorselessly interior, that he seems to shame the extrinsic glamour and extravagance of movies.[69]

This highlights the very real problem of his technique. If he is right, then most, perhaps all other filmmakers are wrong.

So, in summary, actors, imitate other people. Or *try*, in the best way they can, to convey emotions, to express things (following the wishes of the director) or perhaps even not to express things. And the mark of a great film actor is one who can do these things effectively. We are given interpretations by the actors, points of view, opinion, information. We are being manipulated. And yet, from Bresson: "Model. Preserved from any obligation towards the art of drama".[70] The model just lives before our eyes, as expressionless as the viewer. And: "Model. Closed, does not enter into communication with the outside world except unawares".[71] And this is how we experience it, indeed this is how it is in the world, one feels that there is truth here. Bresson gives his models life, but once living they are their own men and women, being themselves, not pretending to be someone else. Yet it is the director who creates them, they are his work and his work alone.

While Andrei Tarkovsky was happy to use actors, he writes:

When I make a film, it is ultimately I who answer for everything, including the actors' performances. In theatre the responsibility of the actor for his achievements and failures is immeasurably greater.[72]

So, straight away we can see the differences. He talks, without embarrassment, of actors and performance. But he restricts the creative input of the performers. The actor, for example, should not know what is to happen, what the whole plan of the film is. If he is aware of the way the film is going to go, so Tarkovsky thinks, then the performance will be different. He, like Bresson, knows that film is very different from theatre: "Cinema has none of the spell of direct contact between actor and auditorium which is so strong in theatre. And so cinema will never replace theatre".[73] For him cinema is a nostalgic medium, it resurrects the same action. Each time we see a film we see the same events, we may see them differently, but the film is the same, the same snatches of time. But in the theatre a play can develop, change and of course, no

---

[69] Thomson (1980), p. 68.

[70] *Ibid.*, p. 53.

[71] *Ibid.*, p. 93.

[72] Tarkovsky (1996), p. 139.

[73] *Ibid.*, p. 140.

performance is exactly the same. Film is more like a record of life, imprinted in time. And the actors in the film are a part of that, as are the sounds, the objects, fire, water, wind, animals. One must remember that for Tarkovsky as for Bresson, films are so much more than the people who populate them: "No one component of a film can have any meaning in isolation: *it is the film that is the work of art*".[74] So everything, from music ("It isolates your film from the life of your film (musical delectation)"[75]) to a literary script, distracts the viewer. Think of a "non-filmic" script, for example, written by another, without the vision of the director. The scenario must be the director's or share his world-view (at any rate it must be assimilated into the film: "The scenario dies in the film"[76]). A film with powerful performances fractures the whole, we are watching acting, theatre. Of course theatre relies on the actors performances. Without acting there is no theatre. For in a play performed (rather than read), the actor is creator. Like Bresson it would be absurd to say of Tarkovsky that he disapproves of theatre, for he writes: "There is nothing more sublime than that unison of actor and audience as they create art together".[77] A film lacking such performances has greater power. One can see why Tarkovsky admired Bresson: "All creative work strives for simplicity, for perfectly simple expression; and this means reaching down into the furthest depths of the recreation of life".[78] Free of distraction, the pursuit of truth is through simplicity, for life is simple and truth here is showing life as it is. Like the sound, music, camera movement, the acting can betray the director's intentions, or rather can make explicit what should never be said: "I am always sickened when an artist underpins his system of images with deliberate tendentiousness or ideology. I am against his allowing his methods to be discernible at all".[79] Tarkovsky himself has been at fault here. He describes what most would think of as a subtle, very moving scene from *Mirror*. The heroine, sick and tired, is

> shot in close up at high speed for the last ninety frames, in a patently unnatural light [...]. We are plunging the audience into the heroine's state [...]. We deform the actress's face independently of her [...]. We serve up the emotion we want, squeeze it out [...]. Her state becomes too clear, too easily read.[80]

---

[74] *Ibid.*, p. 114.
[75] Bresson (1986), p. 76.
[76] Tarkovsky (1996), p. 134.
[77] *Ibid.*, p. 140.
[78] *Ibid.*, p. 113.
[79] *Ibid.*, p. 109.
[80] *Ibid.*, p. 110.

At times one feels, however, that he *has* gone too far, certain scenes in *The Sacrifice*, for example. And yet haven't they all and don't we forgive them? (This isn't altogether true, don't forget Flaubert, Proust, Whistler, Basho, Issa etc) Importantly, the theatre actor builds up his role within himself. For Tarkovsky this cannot be part of film, for in a film the actor simply cannot decide for himself how he should speak, how he should deliver his lines (though he often does), how to interpret the role. This will fracture the film, it will no longer be a unified whole, a director's film. And of course he cannot because he does not know (or should not know) how all the different bits of the film will come together: "His task is to live!-and to trust the director [...]. The director selects for him moments of his existence that express the conception of the film most accurately".[81] So, Tarkovsky felt very strongly that the actor should not connect any scene he plays with the whole film. His actors often didn't know what was coming next or what had gone before, which is how it is in the world. In one early scene of *Mirror*, Margarita Terekhova is waiting for her husband to return. He doesn't, but she hasn't been told this. She is as much in the dark as we are. But this way of working caused real problems, for example, with the leads in *Solaris*, particularly Donatas Banionis, who was very much an analytical actor, from a theatrical background and who never truly came to terms with the approach. Tarkovsky cannot accept actors who will not obey the rules he lays down, who try to direct their own parts, outside the context of his film. They must accept the rules, with ease. They must have childlike trust in the director. They should not ask the questions that theatre actor asks: "Why? What for? What is the key to the image? What is the underlying idea?"[82] The more analytical actor tends to analyse the film as a whole and tries to fit his role into it. Unlike theatre, film "records personality from a mosaic of imprints on film, brought by the director".[83]

He fully approves of Bresson's technique with his models. And for him the performances in Bresson's films will not date, and the same can be said of the films themselves: "Here is nothing calculated or special in their performances, only the profound truth of human awareness within the situation defined by the director. They do not play personae but live their own inner lives in front of our eyes".[84] In Bresson's films there is intense feeling, whether it's unhappiness or joy, but because the models are reduced to automatons they never directly express such feelings, never try to convey how much suffering they are experiencing. Nothing crude is given. The characters are truly themselves, as conceived by the director and thus have nothing in common with theatre, or, as

---

[81] *Ibid.*, p. 140.
[82] *Ibid.*, p. 145.
[83] *Ibid.*, p. 148.
[84] *Ibid.*, p. 151.

Bresson would put it, filmed theatre or cinema. Tarkovsky is perceptive in his observations here. Not only does the character Mouchette never show the audience how terrible her situation is, she doesn't even appear to suspect that her suffering is being observed. She just lives. She simply "is", within her own world. This applies to all his characters. She is there, experiencing her sorrow before our eyes. Notice in the suicide scene, there is no expression of suffering, even of awareness that she is about to die. She waves at a farmer on a tractor, but he appears not to see her (or does he?). For the most part films in general, both those considered 'serious' art and commercial works, hang on doggedly to outdated techniques of acting that should only exist in theatre. For with actors who act (what is often nothing more than cliché) one understands exactly what is going on, one knows what they are trying to do. The audience is told exactly what is going on, what to think, where to laugh or cry. As subtle as those who grin broadly when telling a joke. There is less chance of imagination being stimulated, of thoughts and feelings being evoked, the audience is not given the opportunity. A telling statement from Tarkovsky: "What the audience deserve is respect, a sense of their own dignity. Don't go blowing in their faces; that's something even cats and dogs dislike".[85] Some of this comes down to a desire to please an audience, but once you start to make such concessions there is nothing to be done. An image might seem right, it might follow on appropriately from events, but it is still cliché, expected, it is giving the audience what it wants: "For an actor to be effective on the screen it is not enough for him to be understandable. He has to be truthful. What is truthful is seldom easy to understand".[86]

Film should be a record of facts. He writes: "film is born of direct observation of life; that, in my view, is the key to poetry in cinema. For the cinema image is essentially the observation of a phenomenon passing through time".[87] As is the best poetry, painting, the best art. The different elements, taken from the world and combined into a unified whole: people, objects, animals, the stuff of everyday life, transformed into art, truth. Thus cinematography (or film as observation) doesn't, cannot come close to commercial cinema. Timeless, of a simplicity incompatible with film as it is, it serves as a reminder that while nothing can compete with the power of the Hollywood style (the star system, actors as producers, film by committee), film *can* be placed in the tradition of great art, of poetry, painting and music. That it is not just pretty faces and easy sunsets. (Remember : "The sun blares – and the wind blows from the East – the sky is bereft of cloud [...] the holiday maker rejoices in the glorious day – and the painter turns aside to shut his eyes [...]

---

[85] *Ibid.*, p. 155.
[86] *Idem.*
[87] *Ibid.*, p. 67.

how dutifully the casual in Nature, is accepted as sublime, may be gathered from the unlimited admiration, daily produced, by a very foolish sunset"[88]) These directors *show* us or evoke beauty where the less talented tell us or attempt to reproduce what is beautiful. The implications for cinema, however, hardly bear thinking about.

---

[88] Whistler (1994), p. 85.

References

Bellow, S. (1987). *More Die of Heartbreak*. London: The Alison Press/Secker and Warburg.

Bresson, R. (1986). *Notes on the Cinematographer*. London: Quartet Books.

McNeill Whistler, J. (1994). *Whistler on Art*. Manchester: Carcanet Press.

Tarkovsky, A. (1996). *Sculpting in Time*. Austin: University of Texas Press.

Thomson, D. (1980). *A Biographical Dictionary of the Cinema*. London: Martin Secker and Warburg.

CHAPTER FIVE

THERE IS NO PARADOX OF HORROR

MARK C. RAINEY

In David Hume's classic paper *Of Tragedy* he argues that "it seems an unaccountable pleasure, which the spectators of a well-written tragedy receive from sorrow, terror, anxiety, and other passions, that are themselves disagreeable and uneasy". Although he speaks of well-written tragedy the same may be said of well-made horror films. This notion that sorrow, terror and anxiety are somehow negative emotions has given rise to the 'paradox of horror', according to which it is impossible to actually enjoy negative emotions, and yet people claim to enjoy watching gruesome horror movies which are designed in order to terrify, horrify and revile the audience. So the audience seems to *enjoy the unenjoyable*. When stated in this manner the problem is indeed paradoxical, and so we must explain how (or if) it can be true. I will argue that there is no paradox involved in enjoying well-made horror films.

From an epistemological point of view, in order to make the paradox of horror understandable, there seem to be two obvious solutions; either people do not really enjoy these emotions which are invoked by the horror film, or negative emotions are not unenjoyable. In this paper I will look at Noël Carroll's account of how people can actually enjoy horror films despite the 'unenjoyable' emotions. I will also look at criticisms of his theory from Berys Gaut, who believes it is possible to enjoy fear and disgust. Finally I will present my own explanation of how horror audiences enjoy these films.

Carroll's theory is a cognitive one, and his argument maintains that negative emotions may very well be unenjoyable, but these emotions are not the reason behind our enjoyment of the films. He argues instead that our cognitive interest is aroused by 'the monster' - be it a ghost, an alien, a demon, etc. The reason for our curiosity is simply that the monster is so bizarre and grotesque that we have never seen anything quite like it:

[T]hings that violate our conceptual scheme... are things that we are prone to find disturbing. Thus, that horrific beings are predictably objects of loathing and revulsion is a function of the ways they violate our classificatory scheme.[89]

Basically this means that since we do not see such things in everyday life we are naturally curious to see what 'it' is and how the plot can develop around such a bizarre monster.

For example, we may marvel at how an alien can change shape to mimic any other creature, as in *The Thing*.[90] In this case, and countless others, there is some bizarre monster that violates our classificatory scheme and thus interests us, and we must put up with the horror and fear, etc. as a price to pay for our curiosity. So on Carroll's account, then, a horror film is basically a detective film with a lot of gore; we see a bizarre monster, it kills some people, then the hero discovers its weakness and destroys it. Thus we have been satisfactorily entertained and informed about the nature of the beast, as it were, and if we are to be intrigued enough to sit through the whole film, then the conclusion must be worth the revulsion we experience along the way.

My main doubt about this theory is expressed by Berys Gaut and is simply this; not all horror movies feature a cognitively interesting monster – a "deviation from the paradigms of our classificatory scheme".[91] In many horror films the villain of the piece is simply a human; perhaps a human with a machete or a big hook, but a simple human nonetheless. In a film like *American Psycho* the so-called monster is a Wall Street-style yuppie who likes the music of Huey Lewis and eats at expensive restaurants. This does not violate any classificatory scheme. Carroll calls these films (generally of the so-called 'slasher' genre) "tales of terror"[92] and so he believes that they do not fall into the paradox of horror. This is a fairly weak response, and simply raises a "paradox of tales of terror"[93] since these films still engender the same emotions as horror films.

Carroll may have another response to this by saying that even though the villain, Patrick Bateman, is a fairly uninteresting character most of the time, aside from his sporadic psychotic episodes, our curiosity is still piqued by his activities. So although Bateman is not a classic 'monster', he is still a monstrous individual who does indeed arouse our cognitive interest in the way in which Carroll describes. Poppy Z. Brite, renowned horror author, suggests: "we need to know our monsters, particularly if they are human".[94] This idea suggests that

---

[89] Carroll (2004), p. 283.
[90] I am referring here to John Carpenter's version of *The Thing*.
[91] Carroll (2004), p. 286.
[92] In Gaut (2004), p. 296.
[93] *Idem*.
[94] Quoted in Black (1998), p. 153.

by studying 'human monsters' we can come to understand and perhaps cure them, or at least recognise them easily. But even if this were correct, it does not help Carroll's account with reference to a film like *August Underground* where there is barely even a plot, let alone a monster.

Another way of expressing the main problem with Carroll's account is that it fails to answer the simple question: *"why horror?"* (which, interestingly, is the title of his paper). If a normal human can replace the monster then why should we watch horror films at all, rather than a simple, straightforward detective story? Why should we put up with the blood and gore of *American Psycho* when we could enjoy *North by Northwest* if all we want is an interesting plot to follow? Carroll's account of the enjoyment of horror films relies on the monster; otherwise he describes virtually *any* interesting film, and fails to explain what is special about the horror genre.

Gaut's own theory of our enjoyment of horror films fares somewhat better than Carroll's, but still does not go quite far enough in explaining what is special about horror films in particular. Gaut espouses his 'enjoyment theory', which roughly states that we may enjoy horror films because the emotions involved are not unenjoyable at all; we can enjoy being scared and disgusted sometimes. Thus his paper ends with the conclusion: "There is no paradox of horror".[95] He looks at reasons to explain how we can enjoy such negative emotions, but does not seem to come to any solid conclusion to this matter.

He rightly dismisses John Morreall's "control thesis"[96] which states that we enjoy these emotions just as long as *we are in control,* i.e. we can switch off the television or close our eyes to avoid something which is beyond what we want to experience. If I were to be chased through the woods by a cannibalistic maniac with a chainsaw, I would not enjoy the accompanying feeling of terror because the situation is out of my control. However, if one watches roughly the same thing happen to a character on-screen in *The Texas Chainsaw Massacre* then it is possible to enjoy this kind of fear because if it becomes too distressing it can just be turned off.

It is possible that this kind of 'controlled fear' is more enjoyable than real terror, even outside of the world of cinema. For example, people who enjoy skydiving or riding on roller-coasters experience increased heart rates, rapid breathing, and a genuine sense of fear, although they know they are safe and have some control. That is the very nature of their enjoyment. So with horror films, the audience experiences certain forms of physical arousal which are enjoyable, even though in order to achieve that arousal they must put up with some gruesome or terrifying scenes in a film.

---

[95] Gaut (2004), p. 306.
[96] *Ibid.,* p. 299.

However I think it entirely possible that people can enjoy a horror film precisely because they do lose control. A common reaction to such films is that a viewer may be 'glued to the screen' as it were, and find themselves unable to look away, however horrific the film is. Hideo Nakata's *Ring* and *Dark Water* both rely on a slow-building atmosphere which is intended to draw the viewer in to the point where, at the terrifying climax of both films, the viewer simply cannot look away. In the case of both these horror films it is the very loss of control which makes them more enjoyable than the average film. As Gaut says: "if one is enjoying something, then one's attention tends to be drawn irresistibly to it".[97]

It is precisely this desire to be scared *beyond* one's control which I believe is part of the reason some people enjoy horror films. While it may be true that sorrow, terror and anxiety are negative emotions, I do not believe that this makes them completely undesirable. It seems to me that sometimes some people just do want to be scared. This does not mean they want to live their whole life in a constant state of mortal terror, but it does not mean that they cannot stand to be afraid of something. Positive emotional states like hope and joy may be desired at all times, but this does not mean that negative emotions like fear and sorrow are despised at all times.

It is perfectly plausible to imagine that sometimes an audience simply wants to be scared, and if a film does not succeed in producing the expected result then it can be seen as a bad film; it has failed to do its job and so is not a true *horror* film. The reason that said audience enjoys certain films more than others is because these films are more effective in producing the desired effect; namely fear, apprehension or dread. Part of the reason behind this enjoyment is the fulfilment of the desire to be scared, which has been mentioned, but there is also more to it than that. Another reason some people, including myself, enjoy films like *The Evil Dead* is that not only *do* they scare us, but also that they *can* scare us.

Being a relatively rational, intelligent individual, I find it fascinating that any film can produce feelings of terror in its audience when the audience knows very well that the story is not true; that's not real blood, it's corn syrup; and that man's not dead, it's just a dummy. The fact that special effects and camera trickery can produce a pure emotion like terror is fascinating on a level beyond the mere fear of the monster.

Particularly in the case of *The Evil Dead* I find that a good deal of my appreciation of the film comes from admiring the quality of the effects considering the relatively low budget of the film. It is the kind of film which contains a few mistakes and sometimes the plot seems too unrealistic, but these

---

[97] *Ibid*, p. 300.

things can be overlooked when one considers the fact that it is still a scary movie despite the poor acting and cheap special effects. So my enjoyment of this film may be called a *meta-response*,[98] as it is not so much the story as the 'film-as-a-whole' that I enjoy. Carroll considers the idea of meta-responses but sidelines it, not seeing it as central, as I do.

He sees meta-enjoyment of horror as a kind of endurance test, and believes that these tests are rites of passage for adolescent males. He seems to regret that "one must admit that the phenomenon exists"[99] whereas I see meta-responses to horror differently. I believe there are two more important kinds of meta-response to horror films, as well as the kind Carroll bemoans. The one mentioned above (technical appreciation) is what sets well-made films apart from poorly-made films and is thus a key factor to be considered.

This kind of meta-response to horror can be experienced by those who do not even realise it, and in fact if any horror film is to do its job correctly then the technical trickery should *not* be noticed (at least not at first). Consider two moviegoers watching *The Evil Dead*, where Sam is a film student and Bruce knows nothing of cinematic techniques, etc. but enjoys watching movies. Sam may recognise that certain scenes are filmed with the camera at a canted angle, and he notices the use of non-diegetic sound to heighten tension, and so on. He thinks *The Evil Dead* is the best horror film he has ever seen because of its technical merits. Meanwhile Bruce also thinks it is the best horror film he has ever seen because some scenes created a feeling of apprehension, other scenes scared him, and some characters were very frightening.

So both Sam and Bruce enjoy the film but in different ways. Sam experiences the kind of meta-enjoyment I mentioned earlier while Bruce reacts on a more brute level. The important point here is that Bruce's reactions to the film are caused by the clever film trickery which Sam enjoys, but Bruce is unaware of this – this is the mark of a *well-made* horror film. If he were asked to watch it again and explain why each scene was scary he may notice some subtle tricks, but to notice these things is not necessary in order to enjoy them.

I propose another kind of meta-response which is not essential, but common, to many horror films. That is the idea of monsters as metaphors. Often what is truly horrifying in a film is what the monster (or villain, ghoul, etc.) represents, rather than what it is. There are metaphors of motherhood in *Alien*, with the male victim being forcibly impregnated with an alien embryo in his gut before 'giving birth' to it in a grotesque manner. In *A Nightmare on Elm Street* one interpretation sees the killer as a representation of the horror of the Vietnam war; created by one generation (the parents in the movie) who tried to cover it

---

[98] cf. Susan Feagin, in Carroll (2004), p. 291. Feagin's idea of the meta-response is slightly different from mine, but I believe she coined the term.
[99] Carroll (2004), p. 291.

up and forget about it, but it comes back to haunt the next generation of young Americans (the children in the movie). Another horror classic, *Night of the Living Dead*, has been seen as an attack on American culture, as well as a representation of repressed fears and taboos (death and cannibalism, for example) being brought to life on the streets of America in the form of the living dead.[100]

So it seems there may be three explanations as to why people enjoy horror films, or perhaps it should be seen as one explanation in three parts, as they each relate to a different aspect of our enjoyment. Firstly there is the desirable aspect of Hume's "sorrow, terror, anxiety", which is not to say that we all desire these things all the time; rather that some people desire them at some times. One of the easiest ways to experience such emotions is through cinema, and so horror films are created to cater to this desire for terror.

Secondly, there is the aspect which is particular to well-made horror films, rather than actual terrifying situations or even poorly-made horror films. This is the technical side of the filmmaking process which embeds the fear and dread in the film for the audience to draw out. It is important for this aspect to be seen that the film is indeed well-made, as there are any number of bad horror films on the market. I shall not list them all, but generally speaking most big Hollywood blockbusters are not well-made horror.

Thirdly, is the potential for horror films to represent things which cannot be readily accepted in mainstream movies. The fact that everyone has fears is usually ignored, or else an attempt is made to allay those fears in many movies. Only in well-made horror films can we see our fears represented in full colour and surround sound. If we are willing to read between the lines, so to speak, we can often find a profound subtext behind the blood and guts, and it is this depth and symbolism which makes horror films worth watching.

The horror writer Stephen King says: "I recognise terror as the finest emotion and so I will try to terrify the reader. But if I find that I cannot terrify, I will try to horrify, and if I find I cannot horrify, I'll go for the gross-out".[101] Bad horror films tend to go for the gross-out. They feature a lot of blood and gore, with as high a body count as possible, but no real terror, and no meaningful subtext. Well-made horror films will terrify the audience, and are not shown widely but tend to have a smaller, more dedicated audience which seeks them out. Some may say that this shows that the mainstream audience, i.e. *most people*, are not interested in horror films but I think it shows quite the opposite. That there is a dedicated fan-base for these kinds of films shows that people *do* want to see them and *do* want to be scared by them, and I believe this is due to

---

[100] For more, fascinating interpretation of *Night of the Living Dead* see Brottman (1998).
[101] In Neill & Ridley (2004), p. 271.

my three-fold explanation of the enjoyment of well-made horror films.

If the Humean notion that the pleasure these feelings engender is unaccountable were true, then we would indeed have a paradox to solve. However I think it is possible that sometimes people enjoy fear, and sometimes they enjoy sorrow, but not all the time. This pleasure in negative emotions is no more unaccountable than the pleasure we derive from positive emotions. It is perhaps more rare, but no more unusual. In my opinion to see so-called negative emotions as the opposite of 'positive' emotions is to misrepresent them. No emotion is intrinsically good or bad; some are simply more desirable than others. Generally speaking people may desire happiness and shun fear, but this is not a law by any means. So Gaut is correct in saying that there is no paradox of horror.

References

Black, Andy (ed.) (1998). *Necronomicon: Book Two*. New York: Creation Books.

Brottman, Makita (1998). Improper Burials, Unburied Memories. In Black (1998), pp. 139-144.

Carroll, Noël (1998) Why Horror? In Neill & Ridley (2004), pp. 275-294.

Gaut, Berys (2004). The Paradox of Horror. In Neill & Ridley (2004), pp. 295-307.

Neill, Alex & Ridley, Aaron (eds.) (2004). *Arguing About Art: Contemporary Philosophical Debates*. London: Routledge.

Films

Alien, Ridley Scott, 1979, USA

American Psycho, Mary Harron, 2000, USA/Canada

August Underground, Fred Vogel, 2001, USA

Dark Water (Honogurai mizu no soko kara), Hideo Nakata, 2002, Japan

Evil Dead, The, Sam Raimi, 1981, USA

Night of the Living Dead, George A. Romero, 1968, USA

Nightmare on Elm Street, A, Wes Craven, 1984, USA

North by Northwest, Alfred Hitchcock, 1959, USA

Ring (Ringu), Hideo Nakata, 1998, Japan

Texas Chainsaw Massacre, The, Tobe Hooper, 1974, USA

Thing, The, John Carpenter, 1982, USA

CHAPTER SIX

IT'S A WONDERFUL LIFE, BUT WHY?

JOHN F. CATHERWOOD

It's A Wonderful Life (Capra 1946)[102] is commonly thought of as merely a 'feel good' film, because the happy ending leaves viewers uplifted, although often in tears. It is obviously a film about moral issues, and some moral points are made explicitly, but it is the emotional impact rather than the intellectual one that makes the greatest impression. Indeed the explicit arguments are often insubstantial. From the outset suicide is assumed to be wrong as it is "throwing away God's greatest gift," but the film does not rely on religious authority. This argument against suicide is mentioned, but at no time is it used directly against the suicidal lead character, George Bailey. This is not a religious film, and in other respects the film treats theological matters lightly. While God is invoked in prayer, there is a lack of explicit religiosity and little that could be recognised as standard Christian theology. There is a peculiar notion of a hierarchy for angels, who are dead human beings, where Second Class Angels have to earn their wings, and are then given various miraculous powers. Divine intervention in George's case is through the inept workings of Clarence the Guardian Angel, who is only an AS2 (angel second class) and while he has been sent by angelic superiors it is not clear that they are of necessity Christian theological characters.

I believe that this lack of theological rigour, and the non application of the obvious opening argument, is not simply a matter of chance, or sloppy scriptwriting. We should not dismiss *IAWL* as a mere fantasy entertainment or think it is not worth reading any more deeply.[103] While it is often implausible to suggest that a commercial film should be regarded as a philosophical work representing the ideas of one thinker, in the case of *It's A Wonderful Life* we

---

[102] Here forward *IAWL*.

[103] I am here following in the footsteps of Stanley Cavell (1981) who was content to draw on Capra's "It happened one night" (1934) to discuss Kantian ideas of community and metaphysical isolation, claiming that "one would do well to try conceiving of Capra as possessed of as usable a set of intellectual operations as your average primitive mind."

have a film that was explicitly intended as an expression of the ideology of Frank Capra. Capra's films in the 1930's had often put forward similar moral and political themes, but *IAWL* was the first film for 13 years on which he took a writing credit. This was also the first (and only) production of Liberty Films, in which Capra was a partner. He was the producer of the film, and deeply involved in all pre and post production matters, including the editing and scoring process. This film is the exemplar of his "One man, one film" view of film making as Art. Capra stated "I believed one man should make the film, and I believed the director should be that man, I just couldn't accept art as a committee, I can only accept art as an extension of the individual". (American Film Institute, 1979)

It is also clear that Capra was devoted to the story in *IAWL*, and committed to the ideas put forward in the finished film. Jimmy Stewart, who played George Bailey, reported that when Capra first read "The Greatest Gift", by Philip Van Doren Stern[104] he said "That's the story I've been looking for all my life". Stewart quotes him as saying "All that I was and all that I knew went into the making of *It's a Wonderful Life*". (Stewart, 1991)

It has been suggested by Christopher Falzon that Capra is championing "the utilitarian ideal of working for the common good" and that this film is putting forward the suggestion that "the individual's capacity to contribute to the happiness of others is...a reason for thinking that life is meaningful". (Falzon, 2002)[105] This Utilitarian Interpretation implies that, like George Bailey, our lives are "wonderful". No matter what our position in the world, or how ordinary and small and seemingly unimportant our lives have been, if we have added to the sum of human happiness then our lives are worthwhile and should be preserved. However I believe that this commonly accepted interpretation is unjustified, and is inconsistent with the philosophical assumptions and arguments represented in the film. It also fails to be convincing as a reason for George not to commit suicide, and Capra is aware of this.

The film states that George's decision to kill himself is because he is "discouraged". The cure, according to the interpretation above, is the one proposed by Clarence, who we should perhaps remember is described as having "the I.Q. of a Rabbit". George is shown what the world would have been like without him, and it is during this process that Clarence remarks "You see, George, you really had a wonderful life. Don't you see what a mistake it would be to throw it away?" According to the Utilitarian Interpretation, Capra's

---

[104] Stern (1943). Originally a private publication on a Christmas card, it is available in print through Zoetrope: All-Story, Vol. 5, No. 4, and on line at http://www.all-story.com/issues.cgi?action=show_story&story_id=132.
[105] This is not dissimilar to the interpretation presented by Catherine Wheatley in Chapter 7 of this book.

argument is supposedly that if George was to see how much good he has done he would realise that his life is a good thing, and it would be wrong to destroy it, or wish it had never been.

What justifies Clarence's assertion that George has had a wonderful life, and why should this stop him from killing himself?

Seen from the perspective of George Bailey it is hard to see how anyone could say his life was "wonderful". He has throughout his humdrum and parochial existence kept his dreams of being an engineer, of building vast structures and doing "something big, something important". This is indicated by the model of a suspension bridge in his study area at home, but when all seems ruined and he realises that he has wasted his life, that his dreams will never come true, he destroys the model in rage and despair, and turns to suicide. It is hard to blame him. The longsuffering George has suffered long. In childhood he risked his life to save his brother Harry, and lost the hearing in one ear. When unexpectedly his father died he had to take over his father's business. Without him the Bailey Building and Loan would have closed, and Potter, the greedy and callous banker, would have ruled the town. So George gave up the trip to Europe he had always wanted, and then his college career. He passed over opportunities to make a fortune in manufacturing himself, and sacrificed the money saved for his honeymoon to keep the Building and Loan afloat. Now he faces the possibility of imprisonment for fraud (even though he is blameless) as he has taken responsibility for the loss of investors' money.

It is George's constant unhappiness that gives credence at first to the Utilitarian Interpretation. All of the effects that his life had on the world seem to have been for the benefit of other people. Clarence shows him that without George Bedford Falls became Pottersville in which vice and venality were rife, Uncle Billy was in the asylum, his mother was a wizened hard faced shrew, Gower poisoned a family and ended up a drunkard after a long stretch in gaol, Ernie the cab diver lost his wife and lived in squalor, and Violet was a dance hall girl, probably a prostitute, at best "no better than she ought to be". Thus the utility sum of George's life seems to have been positive in comparison to his non existence. George's life has been wonderful, from an impersonal consequentialist point of view. "Wonderful" here meaning morally worthwhile. Yet this seems a perverse meaning to ascribe. George's life is clearly not wonderful for George, no matter how much of a warm moral glow he might get from a review of his past moral triumphs, and no matter how much happiness his life has brought to others.

Of course the cynical may also argue that Pottersville is not so bad (Kamiya, 2001). The fact that the world is a different place without George does not mean that it is clearly a worse place. Potter is certainly happier, and while Ernie is not happy, perhaps his erstwhile spouse is better off. Violet may have a less respectable career, but who knows what happiness she brings to clients who are less satisfied in Bedford Falls. George has made a difference, but in the long run it is not certain that he has made an improvement in utilitarian terms. Pottersville may be preferable to boring Bedford falls, which George has been trying to escape since childhood. What George, and Capra, see as the horrors of Pottersville are after all part of the everyday life in the places that George longs to visit, and we do not have to trust this parochial prejudice. Moreover it is possible that those who had benefited from George's life may have done so unfairly. Potter may be right – the Building and Loan may have created "A discontented, lazy rabble instead of a thrifty working class". While we may think it sad that Martini's quiet restaurant and bar has disappeared, Nick the waiter in Bedford Falls is Nick the bar owner in Pottersville, and the busy night life of the town suggests a greater disposable income all round.

A consequentialist Capra would then have George affirm his earlier suggestion that "it would have been better if I'd never been born at all" and Clarence's strategy would have backfired. However Pottersville is obviously anathema to Capra, and it is clear that George would never make such a judgement, no matter how much extra utility could be shown to have been generated. It seems unlikely then that Capra would endorse a consequentialist theoretical position that would leave this alternative logically possible.

That said, since George is firmly of the opinion that Pottersville is an unhappy place, if we continue to assume that Capra is a consequentialist then George might have to accept that there is a moral imperative for him to accept his fate, and to have lived his life to date. This at least would give him a moral reason to ask to have lived, and in Van Doren Stern's story George (Pratt, in the original) pleaded.

> Change me back—please. Not just for my sake but for others too. You don't know what a mess this town is in. You don't understand. I've got to get back. They need me here. (Stern, 1943)

However Capra's George Bailey is very different from Stern's George Pratt. In Stern's story we may think that "the utilitarian ideal of working for the common good" is explicit although it is married to the non utilitarian eponymous notion that life is the Greatest Gift and that it is wrong to throw it away because such an act would be hubris. However it is also vital to the story that there is no great crisis in the lead character's life. George Pratt's suicidal urges are simply brought about through boredom

> I'm stuck here in this mudhole for life, doing the same dull work day after day. Other men are leading exciting lives, but I—well, I'm just a small-town bank clerk that even the army didn't want. I never did anything really useful or

interesting, and it looks as if I never will. I might just as well be dead. I might better be dead. (Stern, 1943)

This is why Stern's George needs only to be shown that his life has not been wasted. Once he sees what he has achieved in the past he can appreciate his life as it is now and will go on being if he goes back to it. Capra's George is in far greater trouble, and it is not clear from a consequentialist perspective that suicide would be the wrong thing to do at this point.

Clarence's review of George's life, and the vision of what it would have been like if George had never been born, makes no prediction for the future. Even though he has been reminded by Clarence of the good things in his past life, the present bad has not gone away, and the fact that he has lived a wonderfully useful life for others up until now is no indicator that it will continue to be so. While George has had happiness, and he is obviously still in love with Mary and the family which he also adores, and he had in the past achieved many minor victories of which he could be justly proud, he was nonetheless despairing, frustrated and bitterly unhappy. For him to go back to the life he had was to go back to boring low-grade misery and frustration, "cooped up for the rest of [his] life in a shabby little office" with "the dust of this crummy little town" still clinging to his feet. Indeed worse is to come: the threat of "bankruptcy and scandal, and prison" is still present. His death might lead to the best possible consequences, since it would solve several problems that will face George and his family if he does not kill himself. Having recognised that all his ambitions are unfulfilled, and that what little he has will be ruined, George has little future happiness to look forward to. If he kills himself, letting his family collect on his life insurance, he will save his uncle from prison, and the Building and Loan (and all its powerless customers) may be kept from the clutches of the evil Potter.

In addition, while Clarence has shown George how horrible Bedford falls/Pottersville would be without him he as not shown anyone else this vision. The miserable people of Pottersville do not know how good it would be to have George about, and the people of Bedford Falls, who have already been part of a run on the Building and Loan, and who George thinks are ungrateful, have also not been privy to the horrible alternative. Before the vision George was convinced by Potter's words:

Why don't you go to the riff-raff you love so much and ask them to let you have eight thousand dollars? You know why? Because they'd run you out of town on a rail.

If anything his experience of the brutality of Pottersville should convince him more than ever that his fellow townsfolk are capable of turning against him. He fully expects the worst.

That is why Capra's George has a different plea when he returns to the bridge. It is self centred. "Get me back. I don't care what happens to me. Only get me back to my wife and kids".

Of course Potter was wrong. The riff-raff are being rallied by Mary, and do raise the money, no questions asked. They are grateful for all George's help, and have recognized the value of George's life to them. A more convincing argument to present to George would have been for Clarence to simply tell him that his friends had done this and that he need not despair, that there was a solution to the problem of the missing $8,000.00 which did not necessitate his suicide, and that a better future (from a consequentialist perspective) would be one in which he lived on to do more generous deeds.

Admittedly it would have made for a shorter and less interesting film, but I think that this is not the only reason why *IAWL* does not pursue this argument. Instead we may view the film noir Pottersville insert in this film blanc as an extended *reductio ad absurdum*. Capra has the foolish Clarence present the platitudinous and unpersuasive utilitarian argument in order to ridicule it. The idea that "the individual's capacity to contribute to the happiness of others is...a reason for thinking that life is meaningful" is exposed as just another way for the greedy and the lazy to exploit the good and kind. Had the film ended with George going back to Bedford Falls only to find an angry mob that took his life insurance policy and threw him in the river neither George nor the viewer would have been much surprised.

When he stands on the bridge in Pottersville and cries "Clarence! Clarence! Help me, Clarence," George is not a man who has realised that life is good, nor does he care that his life has often achieved good for others. He does not want to get back so that the needs of the town, or even those of his family, will be met. Clarence's strategy, the Utilitarian argument, has utterly failed, and I believe that Capra intended it to be shown as a failure, precisely because he does not support the impersonal utilitarian ideal. He does not support a moral theory that can make the judgement that George's life is good even if it is utterly dreadful for him. Capra is clearly not a consequentialist.

Capra's point is that it is exactly that kind of depersonalisation, the lack of respect for individual human dignity and worth, that leads to Pottersville. For Capra the notion of the freedom and worth of the individual was a central principle. No individual should be sacrificed for the utility of others, no matter how much utility might be achieved. George was driven to suicide, and that is unacceptable, no matter that it might be the best of all utilitarian possible worlds. It is unacceptable not only because of the background religious argument, but also because for Capra

> 'Masses' is a herd term—unacceptable, insulting, degrading. When I see a crowd I see a collection of free individuals, each a unique person; . . . each a story that would fill a book; each an island of human dignity. (Williams, 1973)

Yet these islands are not entire of themselves. In Pottersville George is totally free, as Clarence says

> You've never been born. You don't exist. You haven't a care in the world. No worries – no obligations – no eight thousand dollars to get – no Potter looking for you with the Sheriff.

Yet in this state of ultimate freedom he is also utterly alone. What drives George Bailey back is his own loss. The final straw in Pottersville is when George sees his transformed wife, who does not know him

> Mary, it's George! Don't you know me? What's happened to us?....Mary, please! Oh, don't do this to me. Please, Mary, help me. Where's our kids? I need you, Mary! Help me, Mary!

It is her rejection of him, and the realisation that he has lost not only her and the family he also loves, but that he has also lost all personal identity, that makes him pray "I want to live again. I want to live again". This is a man who has gone past suicidal despair and into a hellish world of non-existence. It is not just that Pottersville is a horrible perversion of Bedford Falls, it is also that George no longer matters. What little self respect he could have mustered is swept away. The only thing that he is left with is life itself, and the basic instincts of survival: the longing for the familiar, and the comfort of home, so that all other considerations and worries are forgotten. He is no longer suicidal because he is no longer worried about the future. Indeed when he returns home he is clearly in some dissociated state. His exuberance and inability to focus on the seriousness of the situation as he says to the Sheriff "I'll bet it's a warrant for my arrest. Isn't it wonderful? Merry Christmas!" are clearly inappropriate.

It is only when the money comes pouring in, the Sheriff tears up the writ and the Bank Examiner makes a donation, that George, and the audience, can begin to smile normally again. It is only then, in the final moments of the film, that Capra reveals his position: in Harry's toast "to my big brother, George. The richest man in town!" In saying "richest" he is clearly not referring to the pile of money in the basket. This is glossed by the explicit message in the book that Clarence leaves for George: "No man is a failure who has friends".[106] Capra said in his autobiography *The Name Above the Title*

> [*It's a Wonderful Life*] was my film for my kind of people. A film to tell the weary, disheartened, and the disillusioned...that no man is a failure! .... that each man's life touches so many other lives. And that if he isn't around it would leave an awful hole. A film that said to the downtrodden, the pushed-around, the pauper, 'Heads up, fella. No man is poor who has one friend. Three friends and you're filthy rich.' ...I wanted to shout, 'You are the salt of the earth. And *It's a Wonderful Life* is my memorial to you!' (Capra, 1972)

Although this notion of dignity is reminiscent of Kant, it comes from quite different sources. It is notable that the word "duty" never appears in the script, and while it is clear that George often chooses to do what he thinks is right, rather than what he desires, in a manner that Kant would no doubt have praised, it is not just because it is right. He chooses the right thing to do because of who he is, out of his own self respect. Capra's views of what is right, as presented in *IAWL*, are a complex mix of conservative but liberal, caring, libertarian individualism, with communitarian leanings that border on the socialist. Of course we may criticise Capra for inconsistency. In the combative world of political theory these disparate elements do not fit easily together: how can one be a Conservative Socialist? An Anti-Capitalist supporter of the American Dream? A Communitarian Individualist? Yet in Capra's films, while these conflicting ideas are all clearly endorsed, they act in generally harmonious fashion as checks and balances to each other. No single position should be allowed to rule unfettered, and discord arises when this is forgotten.

The evils of Pottersville are those of unrestrained capitalism and liberalism that have thrown off conservative morality in the pursuit of money. Potter is greedy, and uncaring, and therefore bad. Violet, in Pottersville, is violent and drunken but only in response to a cruel world. She has fallen because she has given in to the situation, but she is not a bad person. Capra's approach then is a philosophy of moderation, and it stresses the nature of character over time, rather than individual actions. It is perhaps best characterised as a form of virtue ethics. George Bailey is a good man, not just because of what he does, but despite his failings. When he loses his temper and rants at Uncle Billy, the children and the schoolteacher, it is essential that we see him not as a bad person, but as a good man driven too far. These are desperate acts, not deliberate ones. He later apologises to the children, he feels remorse for having upset the

---

[106] A point missed by Gilbert Sorrentino who claims that the real message is "money is everything". Sorrentino (2000).

teacher and accepts the blow from her husband as a just reward, and he accepts responsibility for the missing money.

For Capra, the measure of a man, and the measure of his life, is confirmed by the strength and number of his friends. It was not being reminded of the good that he had done that brings George back from suicidal despair, it is the realisation that he has friends and is held in high esteem. George's life is a wonderful life, because George is a wonderful person.

References

Capra, F. (1972). *The Name Above the Title*. London: W.H. Allen.

Falzon, C. (2002). *Philosophy goes to the Movies*. London: Routledge.

Kamiya, G. (2001). All hail Pottersville! *The Salon Dec. 22, 2001.*

Sorrentino, G. (2000). Things Ain't What They seem: Frank Capra's *It's a Wonderful Life. Context, 2.*

Stewart, J. (1991). Frank Capra's Merry Christmas To All. *Reader's Digest, December 1991*

Van Doren Stern, P. (1943). *The Greatest Gift.*

Williams, R. (1973). *The Country and the City*. Oxford: OUP.

Films

It's a Wonderful Life, Frank Capra, 1946, Liberty Films, USA

Dialogue on Film, A Series of Seminars with Master Filmmakers: Frank Capra, American Film Institute, 1979. Documentary film (Library of Congress, Division of Motion Pictures)

Screen plays

Frank Capra, Frances Goodrich and Albert Hackett, (with additional dialogue by Jo Swerling and Dorothy Parker, based on earlier drafts by Dalton Trumbo, Clifford Odets, Marc Connelly, and the original story by Philip Van Doren Stern), "*It's a Wonderful Life*" Screenplay, 1945, (film by Liberty Pictures)

CHAPTER SEVEN

THE SPECTATOR AS MORAL AGENT: KANTIAN ETHICS AND THE FILMS OF MICHAEL HANEKE

CATHERINE WHEATLEY

What is striking about philosophical approaches to the problem of ideological interpellation in the cinema is the way in which they confine themselves for the most part to questions of epistemology and ontology. While there is a wealth of critical debate surrounding the question of how the cinematic apparatus controls and positions the spectator, little account has been made of the *ethical* implications of the cinema's workings. And yet, as Noel Carroll has pointed out, the very concept of ideological interpellation has "a pejorative force".[107] Ordinarily we do not want our ideas and our thinking corrupted by outside influences, and theoretical writings on the subject of cinematic interpellation are often inflected with moral terms and judgements. There seems to be a place then for an examination of the underlying ethics of ideological interpellation in the cinema, and its place in critical theory.

Film and Ethics to date

Generally speaking, we can divide those critics and theorists who have brought questions of ethics to bear on film studies into two camps. The first of these groups, which I shall refer to as the 'moralist critics', is comprised of a group of academics and critics working within a tradition that we can perhaps say starts with Peter Brooks's *The Melodramatic Imagination* and is best exemplified in this collection perhaps by John Catherwood's analysis of *It's A Wonderful Life*.[108] These critics give readings of specific films, oeuvres and genres – most notably the Hollywood melodrama – that focus on the questions of morality played out within a narrative context. Typical of the approaches they take are Catherwood and Raymond Carney's analyses of Frank Capra's *It's A Wonderful Life* (1946). Both discussions of the film are particularly interested in plot, character and action, and they focuses almost exclusively on the moral

---

[107] Carroll (1983), p. 73.
[108] Brooks (1976).

trajectory of the film's protagonist, George Bailey (played by Jimmy Stewart). Regarding the spectator's relationship to the film, Carney in particular makes the assumption that by watching George's progression through the film, the viewer can 'learn' something about their own sense of moral responsibility as he empathises with the character's suffering and redemption.

In direct opposition to this approach stands the theoretical movement which D.N. Rodowick labels "political-modernism".[109] Taking their lead from the apparatus theory of Christian Metz and Jean-Louis Baudry, advocates of political modernism including Peter Wollen and Laura Mulvey argue that the cinematic apparatus interpellates the spectator watching a film like Capra's, so that he unthinkingly accepts the system of values that the film promotes. These theorists believe then that classic-realist film is morally suspect because it is politically coercive: they claim that by offering a narrative based on principles of unity, continuity, and closure, such films efface the constructedness of the filmic medium and promote an identification with, and unquestioning acceptance of, the fictional world offered by the film, which frequently promotes specific political values. In the case of Hollywood film, political modernist theorists have argued that its system of representation often involves, for example, the objectification of women, the vilification of homosexuals, and the idealisation of capitalist society, which the spectator is persuaded to accept as "normal" or "natural".

Both these approaches to film and ethics – morality criticism on the one hand and political modernism on the other – seem to fall short of a thorough examination of the ethical implications of the cinema's workings. The former involves an excessive focus on plot, psychology, event and interaction *between* the characters: in other words, on the morality *within* the hermetically sealed filmic world, rather than the morality *between* the film and the viewer: in focusing on close readings and textual analyses of specific films, the morality critics ignore the problem of ideological interpellation. The latter approach, on the other hand, conceives of the problem of interpellation primarily in political terms: it is considered to be morally problematic only in relation to the politics that it promotes.

The Kantian Imperative in Interpellation

To gain a clearer idea of what the moral implications of the cinematic apparatus are, we need to separate the theory surrounding ideology critique from its political context. For interpellation poses a moral problem that is more fundamental than the promotion of any particular politics or system of values,

---

[109] Rodowick (1994).

be it capitalist, fascist or communist. The key relations with which ideology critique is concerned are those of activity and passivity, action and belief. These are the same relations that form the basis of Kant's conception of morality: by reframing the critique of interpellation in terms of Kantian ethics we can shed light upon its moral implications.[110]

In his *Foundations of the metaphysics of morals*, Kant describes an "original state of nature", where everyone pursues his or her own desires without constraint.[111] Children exist in this state, becoming moral beings only with the emergence of reason. That reason acts as a balancing force to the pursuit of desire indicates an innate predisposition towards having a morally good character, consisting of an eradicable recognition that we are obligated to respect and obey the moral law. So everyone can be considered to have some moral good in their character by nature. However, Kant argues in the *Foundations*, living a moral life is a constant struggle, for we are always torn between the laws of morality and the allure of pleasure. Pleasure is in almost constant conflict with morality, for in Kant's view most people privately desire to live "lawlessly, outside the fundamental strictures of morality".[112]

Let us consider the similarities between Kant's theory of the allure of the immoral and Stanley Cavell's theory of cinema's appeal. In his discussion throughout *The Claim of Reason* of issues concerning the troubling of epistemic relations to each other and to the rest of the world, Cavell argues that what cinema grants us is not the power of the pornographer but *respite from our complicity in the structuring of the world*: "not a wish for power over creation…, but a wish not to need power, not to have to bear its burdens".[113] In other words, a wish for a return to the original state of nature.

If we liken the original state of nature to the classic realist viewing position, in which the spectator pursues cinematic pleasure without thought for anything else, we can see that, deprived of his faculty of reason, the spectator is like the Kantian child: he cannot be held responsible for his lack of moral engagement with the act of viewing, since he has no power of rational judgement. Why else is cinema-going so often described as an escapist pursuit? When we seek respite from the world, are we in fact seeking respite from our moral obligations?

Kant argues that man can only be a moral agent by asserting his capacity for rational judgement over his instincts and emotions. More specifically, the moral agent must assert his rational awareness of moral duty over his desire for

---

[110] For a more thorough introduction to Kant's theories of moral goodness, see Barbara Renzi's Chapter 8, featured in this collection, on Kantian and Marxist Issues in *I Girasoli* and *La Classe Operaia Va in Paradiso*.
[111] Kant (1990).
[112] *Ibid.*, p. 24.
[113] Stanley Cavell, cited in Scheman (1995), p. 102.

pleasure or happiness. Now, if we accept that the driving force of the Hollywood apparatus is the spectator's desire for cinematic pleasure, and if we accept that the cinematic apparatus causes the spectator to suspend his self-awareness while watching a film (as I believe we must do, although advocates of the cognitive model of film spectatorship such as Stephen Rainey would doubtless take issue with me here), then it seems that one effect of cinematic interpellation is to foreclose the possibility of the spectator acting as a moral agent within the cinematic viewing situation.

If this is indeed the case, then classical realist cinema – whatever its narrative content – is an ethical vacuum. Individual films may assert a particular set of values, but any moral lessons a film might aim to teach at the level of plot are negated by the very way in which it positions the spectator. Since the success of a classic realist text is premised on our inability to make rational judgements while watching it, true Kantian goodness is necessarily inconsistent with the selfish drive for pleasure and the suppression of awareness that characterises the viewing situation of classic-realist film. The only way in which a film's moral content can be consistent with Kantian goodness is if the spectator can consciously assess that morality and make his *own* judgement about it, rather than reproducing the film's moral outlook as a result of being ideologically interpolated. The ability to reason – critical awareness – is then a necessary condition of any kind of ethical spectatorship, and any filmmaker seeking to create a film that positions the spectator morally must break the spell of cinematic illusion.

The political modernists recognised this, and sought a new kind of cinema that engaged the spectator's reason. In order to break with the dominant model of commercial, narrative cinema, these theorists insisted upon a "politics of representation", aimed at recovering forms that resist or contest its transparency and illusionism. Led by the belief that foregrounding the process of signification would draw the spectator's attention to the materiality of the image, Peter Wollen argued in favour of Brechtian techniques that disrupt the unity and transparency of film form, erode identification with the image as real, and block any possibilities for emotional engagement with the film's characters and narrative, thus promoting a critical awareness in the spectator. By identifying forms of signification and spectatorship in Hollywood film as ideologically complicit with a dominant way of seeing and understanding, Wollen promoted an experimental and avant-garde filmmaking, a "counter-cinema" that required a deconstruction of the ideology of film form in order to address political content.[114] The result is a highly self-reflexive body of films. In keeping with the ideological theory that coincides with it, these films are generally very political,

---

[114] See Wollen (1982), especially pp. 92-104.

two classic examples being Godard's Marxist work *Vent d'est / Wind from the East* (1970, made in conjunction with Groupe Dziga Vertov) and Chantal Akerman's feminist *Jeanne Dielman, 23 Quai du Commerce, 1080 Bruxelles* (1976).

Unfortunately, granting the spectator the ability to engage rationally with the cinematic spectacle is not sufficient in itself to situate him as a moral agent. For according to Kant, moral agency depends on the subject's assertion of his reason *over his desires*, and counter-cinema's approach again falls short of allowing the spectator opportunity to make such an assertion, since it denies him any emotional involvement with the filmic text. The films of the counter-cinema movement are at the opposite extreme of the rational-emotional spectrum from Hollywood film. And they can be just as coercive in their use of rational argument as Hollywood films are in their use of emotional manipulation. When watching a classic-realist film, the moral conclusion the audience arrives at – if the film is successful – is generally the one promoted through the ideological apparatus. So watching *It's a Wonderful Life*, the spectator concludes that the ruthless businessman Mr Potter is morally reprehensible, and that family, friendship and community are worthy pursuits and rewards in themselves, for this is indeed the message played out in the film's narrative, with which the audience is coerced into agreeing through emotional effect and the withholding of critical awareness. But when watching, for example, a feminist film such as Akerman's *Jeanne Dielman*, the audience is also coerced into reaching a fixed moral conclusion – in this case that women's everyday experience is indeed worthy of our careful attention – through the effort of intellectual concentration required and unambiguous filming techniques employed.

So it is that classic-realist cinema prevents the spectator from engaging with film rationally, and Wollen's counter-cinema prevents him from engaging with it emotionally. Both prevent the spectator from exercising his own moral judgement, since both are methods of persuasion: one by emotional interpellation, the other by rational argument.

Michael Haneke and the Moral Spectator

An alternative model of film spectatorship can be found in the films of Austrian director Michael Haneke. These films highlight some of the moral problems inherent to both ideological interpellation and its cinematic critique through counter-cinema. At the same time, they go some way towards resolving these problems through their positioning of the spectator. Haneke negotiates a position for himself which lies somewhere in between those of classic-realist and counter-cinema. He uses Brechtian techniques to break the cinematic spell and bring the spectator to rational awareness, but these techniques are used in conjunction with classic-realist techniques that mobilise the emotions. His films do not aggressively oppose dominant Hollywood forms and approaches, nor do they hold themselves at a lofty distance from them. Rather, they make the spectator aware of the workings of the apparatus and of his part in it, as Haneke solicits a complex spectatorial response by switching between the rationalism of political modernism and the Hollywood mobilisation of emotion. This response echoes the Kantian paradigm of morality as the effect of the reason operating upon the emotions.

Haneke's approach to the problem of awareness mirrors that of many makers of counter-cinema. He employs a number of what might be called 'standard' self-reflexive techniques in his films. In his 1997 *Funny Games* the characters wink at the spectator, acknowledge that they are part of a filmic universe, even rewind the action and replay it in order to alter the outcome. Likewise, Anne, one of the protagonists of 2000's *Code Inconnu / Code Unknown* is an actress, and the film's narrative switches between scenes from her everyday life and scenes from her films with no obvious indication of which we are seeing at any one time. Both conceits will be recognisable to anyone familiar with Godard's oeuvre. Elsewhere Haneke employs more subtle (although no more original) devices: "impossible" camera angles which do not correspond to any character's point of view, blank slides between scenes, and long "paused" shots, in which the camera stays static and little or no action occurs on screen. Such techniques serve as an exposé of the ways in which film exercises epistemic control over its audience, breaking the cinematic spell and waking the spectator from his reverie, in much a similar manner to the films of the counter-cinema movement.

In order to move beyond purely epistemic revelation however, Haneke engages the spectator's emotions *as well as* his reason. In *Theorising the Moving Image*, Noel Carroll discusses what he calls paradigm scenarios, embedded in the stories that people create, disseminate and consume.[115] The force of these scenarios lies in the ways that objects and situations are depicted in connection to sets of emotions. Stories provide paradigms of ways of feeling, and it is the ongoing encounter with such scenarios that helps to shape our emotional attitudes. In this context, a film may reinforce, refine or challenge the dominant paradigm scenarios of a culture. On a narrative level, Haneke's films mobilise paradigm scenarios in order to set up expectations of pleasure and established emotional responses though the use of genre formats, classical editing techniques, linear narratives and other classical-realist techniques, which will be undermined through Brechtian techniques on the films' formal level.

Haneke does not seek to promote a certain set of moral guidelines through his films, but rather to illustrate the ethical problems that he sees as arising in

---

[115] Carroll (1996).

philosophy, society and cinema. More than just a narrative moral schema, Haneke's films comprise a certain conjunction of elements, diegetic and non-diegetic, which contribute to their overall moral effects. The narratives of *Funny Games* and *Benny's Video* (1992) focus on very specific social/ethical problems; more complex questions of how man lives morally in the world are approached in *Code Unknown* and *Le Temps du Loup / Time of the Wolf* (2002). Haneke presents each of these situations with little judgement on the part of the camera or the filmmaker, leaving the spectator, positioned as a moral agent, to consider them autonomously. For example, the plot of *Benny's Video* concerns the actions of a young man, who films his seemingly motiveless murder of a school-friend, and of his parents, who help him to conceal his crime. Although the scenario presents us with the material for a series of ethical problems or debates, these questions are not tackled within the film itself, at least not in the way that they might be in a Hollywood film with a similar plot premise, such as Max Ophuls' *The Reckless Moment* (1949).[116] Furthermore, the film's murderer is neither vilified nor justified through camerawork, editing, dialogue or acting. Of equal importance is the fact that none of Haneke's films allow the spectator any closure or catharsis: their endings are left open, so that the cinematic experience is not a sealed experience, finished when the lights go up, totally separate from the reality in which the spectator lives.

Paradigm scenarios are then, as I have stated, established primarily to be undermined through Haneke's use of the Brechtian devices discussed. These devices reveal the spectator's complicity with the filmic apparatus, a complicity that Haneke deliberately encourages. While in the films of Godard or Akerman, Brechtian devices are intended to distance the spectator from the action of a film and thus allow him to survey the film with a critical eye; Haneke uses the same devices not to achieve an effect of objectivity, but to make the spectator's subjectivity count for something. In distancing him from the cinematic narrative in some ways, they bring him rationally closer to the film in others. By reversing Cavell's premise for cinematic pleasure, and making the spectator present to the action on screen, he emphasises the spectator's proximity to cinematic events – a discomforting experience indeed.

The drive for pleasure, set in motion by Haneke's use of paradigm scenarios and classic-realist devices, is ultimately frustrated. This is in itself a disturbing experience. Through television and mainstream cinema, the spectator is used to having the world presented to him as something explicable (and he pays the empires of Illusion more than enough money to satisfy this need of his for

---

[116] The plot of *The Reckless Moment* bears some similarity to that of *Benny's Video*, in that it involves a mother (Lucia Harper, played by Joan Bennett) who, after discovering the dead body of her daughter's lover, hides the body under the assumption that it was her daughter who killed the man.

reassurance): this fact alone makes a narrative style that denies him any such agreement both irritating and productive. But this frustration is transformed into a set of much stronger emotions when the spectator views the film with his newly awakened rational faculty intact and engaged. As soon as the spectator finds himself out on his own, confronted with questions that are raised by the narrative, yet without instantly given instructions for interpretation, he feels harassed and begins to fight against it. A thriller is thus revealed as an ordeal of intense suffering in which one should not want to take voyeuristic pleasure; an erotic melodrama, an excruciating exposure to more detail than we really want to know. The emotions that arise from these revelations are wide-ranging and differ from spectator to spectator: among them are discomfort, embarrassment, shame, sometimes anger. It is not unusual for audience members to walk out of Haneke's films, and in fact the director once claimed that do so would be the only morally correct response.[117]

Haneke's engagement with the spectator on an emotional level is what differentiates his films from those of, say, Godard, or the feminist film-makers, and it is what enables Haneke to re-enact the Kantian crisis in which moral reason impacts on us as human agents with a moral life that is permeated by the emotions. Within the cinema, the spectator's reason – aroused by the use of self-reflexive devices – asserts itself upon the emotions that are usually manipulated by narrative cinema, and which Haneke mobilises within his films. Were Haneke's films purely intellectual exercises, they would not give rise to any moral conflict, for there would be no emotional, instinctual element for the reason to assert itself over. If he were to fail to sufficiently mobilise the emotions, the film would become a thesis film, one that no more provokes internal moral conflict than an academic textbook would. Nonetheless, however persuasive the emotional aspect of an argument is, if the call to reason is not sufficiently strong then the spectator may not feel the conflict between the scopophilic drive and his moral reason to be particularly pressing. There are a number of classic realist films which involve self-reflexive devices at the narrative level. Stanley Donen's *Singin' in The Rain* (1952) stands out as one example; Richard Quine's *Paris When It Sizzles* (1963) another. Both of these films are exemplary of 'safe' self-reflexivity which employ emotive storylines, continuity editing and classic Hollywood montage techniques with such

---

[117] "Richard Falcon: The form you've chosen – interspersing harrowing naturalistic scenes of psychological torture with off-screen violence – appears to provide a closer experience of victimisation for the audience. If we assume most cinemagoers don't take pleasure in real-life acts of violence, either as participants or voyeurs, is leaving the cinema the most appropriate response?
Haneke: Absolutely! Anyone who leaves the cinema doesn't need the film, and anybody who stays does". Falcon (1998), p. 10.

smoothness that all references to film as a construct are totally unthreatening. The spectator subconsciously acknowledges the fact that film is illusory while at the same time remaining unaware of his own part in the filmic institution. That such a situation is possible reinforces the theory that our critical faculties are entirely suspended when watching a classic realist narrative: the spectator does not believe in this situation that film is reality, otherwise such films would be much more jarring to him, but he is not entirely aware that he is watching a film: in fact, he is not consciously aware of anything. A more recent example of the same phenomenon can be seen in Wes Craven's *Scream* (1996). A highly self-reflexive and ironic take on the horror genre, the film employs structures of suspense successfully so that the viewer's critical awareness remains subjugated to the pleasure drive.

The reception of Haneke's films then depends greatly on how successful each one is in attaining equilibrium between emotion and reason such that they are in conflict with one another. *Code Unknown*, for example, has been described as overly intellectual and lacking in emotional engagement by some critics;[118] *Funny Games* has been compared by others to the afore-mentioned *Scream*, with some younger spectators so caught up in its patterns of suspense and stylised violence that they failed to maintain the emotional distance necessary for the position of moral spectatorship for which Haneke aims.[119] But when Haneke does strike the right balance, when the spectator is positioned exactly as the director intends him to be, the emotion he experiences matches Kant's description of respect for the moral law: a complex emotion comprised of two conflicting feelings. It resembles fear of pain, in that it may demand the denial of self-love or the impulse to pleasure; and it resembles love, in that we recognise the moral law as originating in our reason and as being something that we willingly impose upon ourselves. Haneke's denial of standard models of cinematic pleasure and revelation of the spectator's complicity in the cinematic dialectic creates a feeling of discomfort, intensified by the more direct negative emotional response to narrative events. But at the same time the spectator's critical engagement with the text and realisation of his freedom can give rise to a deep sense of intellectual satisfaction.

To conclude then, we can characterise the moral sentiment induced by Haneke's films as the effect of instinctual response occurring *simultaneously with* rational response within the viewing situation. It is the perfect example of what Robert Bresson describes as the "production of emotion obtained by resistance to emotion".[120] From the moment that the spectator is positioned as a moral agent, instinctive response and rational response are dialectical,

---

[118] See Goudet (2002), pp. 23-24.
[119] See Kermode (1998), pp. 44-45.
[120] Cited in Haneke (1998).

combining to induce moral sentiment. Haneke thus mobilises a tension between emotion and reason that perfectly echoes the Kantian conception of how the moral law is felt. The spectator who is rationally aware of his subjective position but nonetheless engaged with the film's events is analogous with Kant's moral subject, and is responsible for his own participation in the act of cinematic spectatorship. Active in the creation of meaning and aware of himself as such, he assumes a radically different position in this model of spectatorship than he does in the Hollywood or counter-cinema models.

This is of course but one way of conceptualising the ethical problem that underlies ideological interpellation, and Haneke's film constitutes just one way of demonstrating how it might be solved. But it opens the paradigm for a systematic inquiry into the ethical implications of interpellation, and an analysis of Haneke's works can hopefully in turn open the paradigm for a new direction for research in the area of ethics and film.

References

Brooks, Peter (1976). *The Melodramatic Imagination*. Yale: Yale University Press.

Carroll, Noel (1983). *Mystifying Movies: Fads and Fallacies in Contemporary Film Theory*. New York: Columbia University Press.

—. (1996). *Theorising the Moving Image*. New York: Cambridge University Press.

Falcon, Richard (1998). The discreet harm of the bourgeoisie'. *Sight and Sound*, *8:5*, p. 10.

Goudet, Stéphane (2002). Code Unknown (review). *Positif, December*, pp. 23-24.

Haneke, Michael (1998). Terror and Utopia of Form, Addicted to Truth: A Film Story about Robert Bresson's *Au Hasard Balthasar*. in Quandt, James (ed). *Robert Bresson*. Ontario: Wilfred Laurier Press.

Kant, Immanuel (1990). *Foundations of the Metaphysics of Morals*, trans. Lewis White Beck. New York: MacMillan.

Kermode, Mark (1998). Funny Games (review). *Sight and Sound, 2:12* pp. 44-45.

Rodowick, D. N. (ed) (1994). *The Crisis of Political Modernism: Criticism and Ideology in Contemporary Film Theory*. Berkeley: University of California Press.

Scheman, Naomi (1995). Missing Mothers/Desiring Daughters: Framing the Sight of Women. In Freeland, Cynthia A. and Thomas A. Wartenberg (eds.) *Philosophy and Film*. London & New York: Routledge, pp. 89-108.

Wollen, Peter (1982). The Two Avant-Gardes. In *Readings and Writings: Semiotic Counter-Strategies*, London: Verso, pp. 92-104.

Films

Benny's Video, Michael Haneke, 1992, Austria

Funny Games, Michael Haneke, 1997, Austria

Code Inconnu / Code Unknown, Michael Haneke, 2000, France

Le Temps du Loup / Time of the Wolf, Michael Haneke, 2003, France

It's A Wonderful Life, Frank Capra, 1946, USA

Jeanne Dielman, 23 Quai du Commerce, 1080 Bruxelles, Chantal Akerman, 1976, Belgium

Vent d'est / Wind from the East, Jean-Luc Godard & Groupe Dziga Vertov, 1970, France

Paris When It Sizzles, Richard Quine, 1963, USA

Scream, Wes Craven, 1996, USA

Singin' in The Rain, Stanley Donen, 1952, USA
The Reckless Moment, Nicholas Ray, 1949, USA

CHAPTER EIGHT

KANTIAN AND MARXIST ISSUES IN *I GIRASOLI* AND *LA CLASSE OPERAIA VA IN PARADISO*

BARBARA GABRIELLA RENZI

Films can illustrate philosophical points very clearly, although this view might appear counterintuitive at first because philosophy and cinema are commonly associated with different activities. If reflection, arguing and debate are the main activities involved in philosophy, they might not be prevalent in films. When we practice philosophy we usually develop arguments and try to think of possible counter-arguments, examples and counter-examples. It can be a very tiring activity. Films, on the other hand, let us relax and while we are watching them, we need not rack our brains in order to come up with original or rigorous reasoning. Philosophy, moreover, is usually associated with the non-figurative and theoretical; films are figurative, concrete and immediate.

I regard this opposition between figurative expressions and philosophy as an illusory although very old distinction. It probably dates back to Plato's myth of the cave, as Christopher Falzon points out:

> Plato's claim is that sense experience only gives us access to shadows. To grasp the real nature of reality [...] we have to break free from dependence on sense experience and use reason alone. [...] This would seem to represent a deep philosophical prejudice against the visual image as an avenue to philosophical enlightenment. And things look even less promising when we consider cinematic images, because the very structure of the modern cinema is reminiscent of Plato's cave.[121]

We are sitting in the dark and we just watch shadows projected on a big white screen, just images and not reality. Falzon points out the whole issue might be considered from a different angle: Plato's 'cave myth' is itself an

---

[121] Falzon (2002), p. 4.

image that serves to illustrate his philosophical perspective, it is an image functional and valuable for philosophy.

Indeed, images have been used by philosophers constantly from Plato's time on. For instance, different kinds of foundational images have been used in epistemology over time. Descartes[122] describes the epistemologist as an architect who wishes to build a house and has to find the basis, the bedrock, on which to lay the foundations of their philosophy. He also describes epistemology as a chain of reasoning, while Charles Peirce uses the image of a cable.[123] One of the most influential images is Otto Neurath's ship,[124] which was popularised by W. V. O. Quine.[125]

Images are not used just in epistemology, they occur in every branch of philosophy and they are used for different goals. Two main uses, however, can be identified: one is to present models, analogues of something (anything from a whole system to a single concept) that needs further explanation. By means of an image, as in the cases just illustrated, some of the properties of the *explanandum* are highlighted by relevant properties of the model image. The second use, instead, aims to exemplify and shed light on philosophical points by ostensive reference. In this case, a realisable example of the *explanandum* is offered and, because of its nature, this use is widely found in ethics and political philosophy. The presentation of an imaginable situation involving moral agents, for example, is an irreplaceable tool for the analysis of ethical questions but also for the illustration of standing points. Here I will briefly show how whole films or fragments, by representing a complexity of actions and interactions of fictitious *egos*, can be very valuable in exemplifying ethical and political philosophy issues.[126] This will be achieved by using two well-known Italian

---

[122] "When an architect wants to build a house which is stable on the ground where there is sandy topsoil over underlying rock, or clay, or some other firm base, he begins by digging out a set of trenches from which he removes the sand, so that he can lay his foundations on firm soil". Descartes (1984), vol. 2, p. 366.

[123] "Philosophy ought to imitate the successful sciences in its methods [...]. Its reasoning should not form a chain which is stronger than its weakest link, but a cable whose fibres may be ever so slender, provided they are sufficiently numerous and intimately connected". Peirce (1958), pp. 40-41.

[124] "We are like sailors who must rebuild their ship on the open sea, never able to dismantle it in dry-dock and to reconstruct it there out of the best materials". Neurath, (1959), p. 201.

[125] "Neurath has likened science to a boat which, if we are to rebuild it, we must rebuild plank by plank while staying afloat in it". Quine (1960), pp. 3-4.

[126] This, of course, does not imply that whole films or fragments of them might point to questions belonging to other philosophical domains such as philosophy of the mind, as the well known phenomenon of *The Matrix* shows. It does not imply either that cinematic products might be seen as metaphors or models of philosophical relevance, as in the first

films: *I Girasoli* (*Sunflowers*) and *La Classe Operaia Va in Paradiso* (*The Working Class Goes to Heaven*). In particular, I am going to argue that the last sequence of *Sunflowers* by Vittorio De Sica (1970) helps us to understand the Kantian[127] conception of morality, while *The Working Class Goes to Heaven* by Elio Perri (1971) illustrates a number of Marxist ideas, especially the concept of 'alienation'.

Kant's ideas on morality

What is 'moral good' for Kant? How can we decide what good is? The indication given by Kant is innovative and he is aware of the novelty of his point of view. In earlier philosophical traditions, *good*, in the sense of happiness, love, pleasure, was thought to indicate what the moral law was. For Kant however, the concept of good or bad cannot be determined prior to the moral law. Furthermore, moral deeds cannot be the pursuit of one's own interest, pleasure, or desires, but they are based on moral obligation (*Sollen*), and its source is reason. Morality is obedience to our own rational conscience and human beings are primarily understood as rational agents. We establish our own rules as we are rational beings: human reason provides the categories by which we systematise our experience and the principles by which we have to organise our moral conduct. The only thing which is good without qualification is good will; everything else (talent, self-control, intelligence) may be utilised to bad ends.

The underlying principles motivating an action establish its moral worth. These principles are called *maxims* by Kant. One of the key terms in understanding Kant's position, is 'good will'. An act of good will is not good because of its effects, but because of the volition which is good in itself and reason as the instrument to achieve it. Different maxims could have the same deeds as a result; for instance, a person might not lie in a certain situation, because they are acting either on the maxim 'always tell the truth' or on the maxim 'tell the truth when it is not possible to lie'. For Kant, however, only the first maxim is a moral one. While maxims are rules that a person has chosen to adhere to, *moral* maxims can be identified thanks to the categorical imperative, which determines the moral law. The categorical imperative[128] is a command and applies unconditionally, irrespective of our aims. There is only one

---

kind of use of images just identified. For example, the film *The Truman Show* might be seen as a metaphor of Plato's cave. However, I will not pursue this analysis here.

[127] On Kantian ethics, see also Catherine Wheatley's Chapter 7, in this collection.

[128] 'Will' means here 'rationally intend', while 'law' refers to moral and not legal law. There are two sorts of imperatives: hypothetical and categorical. A hypothetical imperative has the form 'if you wish to reach a certain goal, act accordingly.'

categorical imperative, the imperative of morality: 'Act only on that maxim through which you can at the same time will that it should become a universal law'.[129] That is, when a maxim is a moral one it should be applicable universally; that is, it ought to apply to everybody in similar conditions. Take the case of the maxim 'do not lie'. The idea behind Kant's position is that you should not lie because it is wrong and not because following this command would help you to reach a certain end. Furthermore, I could not will that everybody should act on the maxim: 'lie', since if everybody lied, the power of lies would not be effective any longer, because trust would be impossible. Moral rules are what each of us, as rational agents, chooses freely; they derive from the use of rationality which guides our will. So, on reflection, we will see why it is rational to follow these rules: our choice is based just on our will and not on emotions.

I find a clear exemplification of the main points of Kantian ethics in the final scenes of *I Girasoli*. The film is set in Italy during, after the Second World War and ten years later. It starts with a sequence of a field of sunflowers, later we apprehend that under those sunflowers rest the bodies of the Italian soldiers who died on the Russian front during the War. The two main characters are Antonio (Marcello Mastroianni) and Giovanna (Sofia Loren). Antonio is to leave in two days for the African front and he agrees to marry Giovanna, whom he has just met, to delay his departure. But from the start it is quite obvious that this is not the only reason.

As the film goes on, we see how strong love and passion between the two are. After a short but passionate honeymoon in their house, Antonio decides to pretend to be insane in order to avoid the war and remain near his bride. Unfortunately his bluff is soon unmasked and he is punished: he is sent to the Russian front. The war ends but he does not come back: Antonio is missing. Giovanna is convinced that her husband is still alive and she determinedly waits for him. Strangely enough, her firm belief is reinforced after encountering a soldier in Antonio's platoon, Glauco. He tells Giovanna about the last time he saw Antonio, too tired to go on during a retreat and sinking into the snow. Nevertheless, Giovanna still believes that Antonio is alive and, despite all the evidence, leaves for Russia. With no indications and no available facts to support her belief, she looks for him in Moscow and in the Ukraine and she manages to find him: he is still alive and he has been living in a small village since the war. He was saved from frostbite by Mascia (Ljudmila Saveljeva), his present partner with whom he has a daughter. After the shocking discovery, Giovanna in despair goes back to Italy and starts a new life: a new boyfriend

---

[129] Kant provides several formulations of this imperative: 'Act so as to treat others and yourself always as ends, never simply means to ends' and 'Act as if through your maxims you were a law-making member of a kingdom of ends'.

and, after a while, a child. Eventually, Antonio, tortured by the episode with Giovanna, goes back to Italy to declare his love for her with the intent to start a new life with her somewhere else. Although Giovanna still loves him, she puts aside her feelings for the moral obligation due to her new family and convinces him to behave morally as well.

One of the commentators of the time (F. Sacchi) defines *I Girasoli* as a film produced for monetary, rather than aesthetic, purposes. On a more positive note he praises De Sica for his ability to create such an emotional atmosphere and Sophia Loren for her talent of touching all the right chords of emotion and feeling. Sacchi is surely right, although I think moral obligation is the key element to interpreting the film in another, more interesting way: the two lovers decide to separate from each other for ever by showing values and strength of character. They take this decision not because of inclination but duty, as the final sequences show.

Antonio travels back to Italy in order to convince her to get back together with him and start a new life. Giovanna is very emotional, still in love, but she controls her desires. She cannot move blindly and be led by her passions; she now has some responsibilities to fulfil and convinces Antonio that the best thing to do is to live their lives separately. *Sunflowers* ends on a strong Kantian note: moral considerations have a special force, which outweigh all the other considerations and feelings, even a love which survived the War.

From their dialogue, distress appears evident in both the characters. At first Giovanna refuses to meet Antonio but eventually, as he is forced to spend the night in the city anyway because of a strike, she agrees. While he is on his way to Giovanna's house, she puts on the earrings that he gave her as a wedding gift. Nature seems to mirror the tempests of their hearts: it is raining in torrents. They meet in the dim light of the apartment, as the storm has caused a power-cut.

After their initial embarrassment, Antonio tries to explain why he never returned home and, although unsuccessfully, apologises:

> If you only knew how difficult it was... One thousand kilometres of snow were ahead of me. When I opened my eyes again I was in an unknown house. I could not remember a thing. And I could not remember anything for a long time. [130]

Giovanna, without anger, points out that he should have thanked the woman and gone back home to her, instead he had decided to stay there and even to

---

[130] "Ma sapessi cosa ho passato. Avevo davanti mille chilometri di neve. Quando ho riaperto gli occhi mi sono ritrovato in una casa che non conoscevo. Non mi ricordavo più di niente. Per tanto tempo non mi sono ricordato più di niente".

have a baby. Antonio explains how he felt: that house appeared to him the only safe place that he had left:[131]

> It was as if I were dead, and afterwards I was somebody else. Being so close to death changes people. It changes feelings. I found a bit of peace with her.[132]

He continues by saying how hard war is and how everything became so difficult, and he really does not know why things happened that way and he truly does not know why he did not go back to Italy.

After having apologised and declared his love, Antonio asks Giovanna to get back together with him, since he still loves her and he knows that she feels the same way; Giovanna looks lost and repeats four times: "But how can I possibly come back to you?"[133]

In the scene where they kiss, it emerges how passion is not just still alive but also strong. However, during their kiss Giovanna's baby starts crying and her look changes: "I have a baby. Do you understand now, Anto'?"[134]

Antonio is not convinced: "But I cannot leave like this. I'll bring you with me. We'll start a new life somewhere".[135]

She is suffering, we can witness the struggle between her moral obligation and her feelings but the voice of reason prevails and guides her. She distinguishes between her duty (towards her son) and her pleasure and chooses to be moral. She also forces Antonio to understand: "Where would you bring me with this baby ... young, so young?"[136] Her sense of duty outweighs all other considerations. The day after these events, Antonio leaves Milan. She cannot hide her distress and cries with pain, probably finally mourning his death.

For Kant, the moral is experienced as a voice of duty, which commands us to put pleasure aside and do the right thing and that is what Giovanna does when she chooses to send her former lover, the love of her life, away. When we are acting out of a sense of duty we are acting in accordance with our rationality and to be moral is to act in accordance with principles which are binding for rational beings. Reason is what raises human beings above all other creatures. We

---

[131] Antonio decides to go back to Italy when he had to move with his family from the little village in Ukraine where they used to live to an apartment in a big city.
[132] "È stato come se fossi morto e dopo ero un altro. La morte così vicina cambia le persone. Cambia i sentimenti. Io con lei avevo trovato un po' di pace". Antonio is referring here to Nascia.
[133] "Ma come torno con te?"
[134] "Ho un bambino. Hai capito Anto'?" Anto' is the short version of *Antonio*.
[135] "Ma non ti posso lasciare così. Ti porto con me. Ci rifaremo una vita da qualche parte".
[136] "E dove mi porti con questa creatura… piccola piccola?"

should control our yearning and live up to what we are, rational agents and this is what Giovanna does. If we were moved only by our emotions or feelings, we would not live up to our rationality. Reason serves to produce a will, which is good not as a means to further end, but in itself. To act rationally is to exhibit good will in difficult situations. Being rational implies a continuous battle against our passions and feelings, and Giovanna wins her battle and acts morally.

Kantian ethics is bound to the notion of freedom, as ethical human beings observe rules that they have formulated for themselves. By obeying our own rules we are free from nature, desires and inclinations, and authorities such as churches or similar institutions. This is also exemplified in Giovanna's actions, she freely decides to fulfil her obligations to her new family although she is breaking an external rule: according to the Italian law she is still married, to Antonio. This external, formal bond does not influence her decision, nor her feelings.

I *Girasoli* is a film about passion and human feelings, all revolving around the internal struggles of the characters. Although the War is the actual source of all their troubles and sufferings, its deadly face of mass destruction is only shown very briefly as a backdrop. Equally, other collective events are just thrown in as significant background, such as the mass urbanization of Soviet Communism, which triggers Antonio's desire to go back and see Giovanna. Or the socio-political tensions and instabilities of the Italian industrial boom, echoed by the rail strike that forces Antonio to stay in Milan for the night. Symmetrically, in *La Classe Operaia va in Paradiso*, shot only one year later, the social struggle of conflicting classes is analysed from several perspectives while personal events, although not exactly in the background, are almost used as mere exemplification of the Marxist doctrine as it was interpreted in the explosive Italian society of the late 60s and 70s.

Marx and Alienation

Marx was influenced by Hegel's belief in the laws of history. Hegel maintains that history is led by laws whose nature is spiritual, while Marx considers them material,[137] because their nature lies in economy. Property and power are the two crucial points around which society is structured: changes in society are not led by ideas, but by force alone. According to Marx, even though Utopians believe that society can be modified by ideas, they are mistaken in

---

[137] Marx was also influenced by Feuerbach, who maintains that the spiritual realm is a myth created by humankind, because of human being's dissatisfaction with their present condition and their need to believe in a future improvement.

thinking that human beings' actions are motivated by ideas: the economy and the means of production still structure the rest of society, as they did in the past.

For Marx and Engels, the development of history is regulated by laws, which are inexorable and economic in nature. The social, political and spiritual processes of life (superstructure) are determined by the mode of production of material life (substructure). Technological changes determine social change: everything (also dominant ideas) is due to the distribution of social goods. Every new technology changes society and its dominant ideology. As technology changes continuously over time, society is never stable and so ideas, which are the reflections of economic interests and the tools by which the ruling class strengthens its power, change as well.

Human nature is neither timeless nor static: we are the result of the economic conditions of our time, which shape our lives and thoughts. The historical circumstances shape who we are.

In Chapter 15 of *Das Capital*, Marx points out that technology not only plays a fundamental role in our society, but that its influence will grow more and more, while serving the capitalistic interest, and not that of the worker. He focuses on the extreme division of labour (in particular the intellectual and physical division) which has a powerful negative influence on what human life can be, giving rise to alienation (the distancing of individual labourers from their life). The division of labour renders individuals 'slaves of the system' and dehumanises them: dull and harsh physical work diminishes their possibilities of achieving a fulfilling life. This very last concept is highlighted throughout the film I have chosen, although more in some sequences than in others.

The main character of *La Classe Operaia va in Paradiso* is the factory-worker Ludovico Massa,[138] shortened to Lulù. He works in a factory producing mechanical components and he is a sort of champion of 'piecework': his productive rhythm is the best and nobody can equal his productivity. Lulù himself acknowledges his ability when he describes himself as 'il campioncino' (the little champion) of the factory. He has won his employer's affection, but he is disliked (or even hated) by the other workers. The main reason why his fellow workers cannot tolerate Lulù is that their employer benchmarks everybody's productivity against Lulù's. The management remodels the time of production on his productive rhythm and then imposes these standards on the others. A sequence of the film shows how Lulù is asked to work on each different machine, while one of the inspectors registers his time of production, which is usually remarkable. In one case, Lulù explains to one of his fellow workers what movements he has to undertake in order to save fifteen seconds in the

---

[138] His surname 'Massa' might mean 'a multitude of people'. Is it referring to the start of the rampant globalisation of the individual?

production of each mechanical piece. This is a clear reference to the spread of 'Taylorism', which applies 'scientific work management' to the workers themselves, by organising their whole series of movements in order to obtain the maximum efficiency. From a Marxist point of view, the worker becomes a component of the machine as his movements become fully standardised and dictated by the necessities of the production.

After Lulù's performance the worker assigned to that machine is asked in quite a stark manner, and without discussion, to conform to Lulù's rhythms. His fellow workers, quite understandably, neither like nor respect him:

> *A fellow worker*: Look Lulù, you won't have a peaceful death, do you know that? You are going to die here, on the machine![139]
> *Lulù*: I don't care...

Notwithstanding this answer, Lulù is not pleased with himself. He works very hard and buys all the latest things, but is killing himself with fatigue. He owns a car, a TV and his house is full of useless objects but he is working himself to death. He returns home so tired that he has no energy left to make love to the woman he lives with. (Lidia, played by Mariangela Melato). Lidia complains about this situation quite often and he tries to defend himself. [140]

> *Lulù*: What do you think, that I am looking for excuses, do you think that I am looking for excuses? But what do you think, that I have a machine here, between my legs?
> *Lidia*: Ah, I cannot even remember it!

After a few lines he admits that he is too tired to have sex:

> *Lulù*: Look, I feel like it just in the morning... not in the evenings. In the morning, when I enter the factory, I could have sex with three women.
> *Lidia puffs*.
> *Lulù*: But you are not there. You are at the shop. At the shop, well... In the evenings I don't feel like it, maybe I am too tired. But would you try to understand, damned bitch, that in order to have some money I work my butt off. And they attack me, they tease me, they challenge me and you don't know what I have to bear, I am lonely and miserable.

Lulù continues working at his self destructive pace until an accident at work happens, caused by tensions between him and the other workers, and he loses a

---

[139] "Senti Lulù , te non muori mica nel tu' letto sai? Te mori qua, sulla macchina!" "Indifferente...".

[140] See below, Dialogue A, for the original dialogue.

finger. After the accident he changes completely. He is not the perfect worker any longer, who agrees with whatever the employer says. He changes so much that he gets involved with the extreme left. He supports the necessity of an all-out strike and the day after a violent demonstration of workers at the factory, he is fired for political reasons. He is left alone, with no skills and no hope of finding another job. After a period of solitude and desolation, having been deserted by his partner and by the extremists, he receives some good news: his partner comes back home and thanks to the intervention of the trade union he gets his job back. Notwithstanding the good news, he returns to work in a mood which is melancholy and probably on the verge of madness.

The last sequences of the film are surreal and bitter. Lulù tells his workmates his recent and strange dream: a wall is knocked down and beyond the wall there is fog, not paradise for the working class as he was expecting, but just other workers condemned to work.

This film centres on work in the factory, social injustices, and the rare solidarity among the workers, but it is above all a Marxist film, which exemplifies some of the key concepts of Marxist philosophy.

At the beginning of the film Lulù wakes up before the alarm clock rings, prepares coffee for himself and for Lidia, jokes with his stepson about football and then brings the coffee to Lidia, who is still in bed and the following are the first words that he exchanges with her that day.[141]

> *Lulù*: Everything is in here... [*He touches his head*] in the brain there is the central direction, it decides, it plans, programmes and it starts production...the arms, the legs, the mouth, the eyes, the tongue, everything starts moving until the food is grasped, which is the raw material.
> *Lidia*: What are you talking about?
> *Lulù*: First: the individual works to eat.
> *Lidia*: What a discovery!
> *Lulù*: The food goes down and here [*he points to the stomach*] there is a machine that... Crushes, and everything is ready for the exit!
> *Lidia*: What?!
> *Lulù*: The individual is identical to the factory.
> *Lidia*: And so what?
> *Lulù*: FACTORY OF SHIT!
> *Lidia* Ah shit, shit, shit... What kind of language in the early morning! [*she looks very annoyed!*]
> *Lulù*: ...But look, please, reason...
> *Lidia*: You reason, instead of me!
> *Lulù*: Think if shit could be sold, right? Everybody could easily have their small, guaranteed income... on the contrary we don't know where to place it...

---

[141] See below, Dialogue B, for the original dialogue.

These lines share Marx's and some German neo-Marxist worries: the workers become simple components of the machine or machines themselves, cogs in the process of the production. Right from the start, the film portrays the dehumanisation of the worker, the individual as a machine, and the only thing he is able to produce autonomously is worthless. This dialogue is also a metaphorical illustration of Marx's account of industrial labour. The fruits of production are due to the manual workers. The theory of surplus points out that only a part of these fruits are given to the proletariat, just the minimum required to enable the proletariat to continue working. Their tiring work has, as a result, an almost worthless income.

Some sequences later, while he is showing how to operate a machine to two newly arrived workers, Lulù's actions are accompanied by the following words: "This is a job that even monkeys can do".[142] Again, it is pointed out that the skills of the worker are taken over and the worker is fully degraded. The same idea is confirmed when Lulù, in the canteen with the newly-hired workers, is asked how he manages to be so quick and produce so much.

He replies:

> In the factory I get bored, it gets on my tits, so I work, right? I work, what should I do? Look at my concept. Life: finishing line, banner, everybody is on the track, here we are all in competition, I am a little champion here… I focus…I have a technique to help me focus […] I think of her ass…[143]

The work is so monotonous and boring that one needs no concentration in order to perform it; Lulù just focuses on something enjoyable and totally unrelated in order to continue the repetition of these same movements.

After his accident Lulù goes to speak with his friend Militina (Silvio Randone). From their dialogue it is evident that alienation can be so serious as to cause insanity, as happened to his old work-mate. The capitalist controls the work, since they own the machinery whilst the worker is unable to understand the meaning of the work he does. The individual is reduced to an appendix of a machine and does not need to think. The dialogue takes place in a mental hospital, where Militina is living. Lulù is worried that he is going down the

---

[142] "Questo qui è un mestiere che puó fare anche la scimmia".

[143] "È che io in fabbrica mi annoio, mi rompo i coglioni, allora lavoro no? Lavoro, cosa devo fare? Senti il concetto. La vita: traguardo, striscione, tutti dentro in pista, qui dentro siamo tutti in corsa, io sono un campioncino qui dentro...
Sono concentrato... io ho la tecnica per concentrarmi, lei lo sa: mi fisso col cervello... penso a un culo, il culo di quella lí...".

same road, and asks Militina how he realised that he was going insane. He tells him that 'the others' decide for you and, adds:[144]

> *Militina*: Would you like to know what the fuck we manufacture in that factory? [...] How all these pieces that we manufacture in millions are going to be used?
> *Lulù*: I know it, I know it, I produce pieces that will be used in an engine..., which is used in another machine, which is not there, it is not there.

Lulù does not really understand what he is producing, or his own function in the process. This is a typical example of Marx's concept of alienation in a technological society. Militina explains to Lulù: "...this, Lulù, is not madness, because a human being has the right to know what he is doing and what he is useful for."[145]

When Lulù gets his job back, one of the leaders of the Union points out it was the first time that a worker, fired for political reasons, was re-employed in that part of the country. His attitude and the rest of his speech illustrate a further point in Marxist philosophy: an ever-diminishing bourgeoisie is confronted by an ever-increasing proletariat. Workers are becoming conscious of their strength; society is ripe for the proletariat. The Union does not advocate a violent resolution. The revolution is encouraged by the numerous acts and speeches of the extreme left. 'To capitalist violence, you answer with proletarian violence',[146] is what is regularly shouted by the members of the extra-parliamentary left at the opening and the closing of the factory.

The Working Class Goes to Heaven clarifies by exemplification some Marxist criticisms of capitalist society, such as workers living an impoverished and alienated life; they are servants of technology while the latter should serve human needs. It portrays the lone worker coping with a mechanical world, subordinated to his role in the system of production.

---

[144] See below, Dialogue C, for the original dialogue.
[145] "... questa, Lulù, non è pazzia, perché un uomo ha il diritto di sapere quello che fa, a che cosa serve...".
[146] 'Alla violenza dei padroni si risponde con la violenza proletaria'.

Dialogues

Dialogue A

Lulù: ... cosa cerco le scuse io, cosa cerco le scuse io? Ma cosa credi, che tengo una macchina qui, in mezzo alle gambe? ...
Lidia: Ah, io non me lo ricordo mica! [...]
Lulù: Sai cosa ti dico? Che a me mi vien voglia solo al mattino [...] La sera niente. Al mattino, quando entro in fabbrica. Me ne farei anche tre.
Lulù: Ma te non sei mica lí. Sei al negozio. Al negozio, insomma... eh! La sera niente. Io non so, sarà la stanchezza. ... Ma lo vuoi capire, brutta porca maledetta, che io per tirar su 20 carte in più al mese mi faccio un culo così? E mi attaccano, mi sfottono, mi contestano e so solo io quello che soffro, come un cane, guarda, come un cane...

Dialogue B

Lulù: Tutto qui, il cervello... nel cervello c'è la direzione centrale, decide, fa i progetti, i programmi, e dá il via alla produzione... l'individuo... l'individuo entra in pista, si mette in movimento... i bracci, le gambe, la bocca, gli occhi, la lingua, tutto, mette in movimento e... finché non... agguanta il cibo, che è la materia prima.
Lidia: Ma che cos'è che dici?
Lulù: Uno: l'individuo lavora per mangiare.
Lidia: Bella scoperta!
Lulù: Il mangiare viene giù e qui c'è una macchina che ... schiaccia, ed è pronto per l'uscita, uguale che è in una fabbrica!
Lidia: Eh?!
Lulù: L'individuo è uguale ad una fabbrica.
Lidia: E allora?
Lulù: FABBRICA DI MERDA!
Lidia: Ah merda, merda, merda.... con questo frasario qua di mattina presto!
Lulù: ...Ma senti scusa, ragiona.
Lidia: Ragiona te piuttosto!
Lulù: Pensa se avesse un prezzo, eh? Ognuno lì bello, con la sua renditella sicura...Invece niente, non si sa dove metterla...

Dialogue C

Militina: A te ti piacerebbe sapere che cazzo fabbrichiamo nella fabbrica, [...] a che servono tutti questi pezzi che fanno a milioni?
Lulù: Io lo so, io lo so, io faccio dei pezzi che servono per un motore ... questo motore che va a finire in un'altra macchina, che però non è lì, non è lì.

Acknowledgements

Thanks to Ryan Sympson, Lucy Bolton, Mary Alice Clancy and Michael Reinsborough for their comments on earlier drafts of this paper.

References

Descartes, R. (1984). *Philosophical Writings of Descartes*. Cambridge: Cambridge University Press.
Falzon, C. (1974). *Philosophy Goes to the Movies*. London: Routledge.
Kant, I. (1973). *Critique of Pure Reason*. London: Macmillan Study Edition.
— (1998) *The Groundwork*. Cambridge: Cambridge University Press.
Marx, K. and Engels, F. (1975). *Collected Works*. London: Lawrence & Wishar.
Neurath, O. (1959). Protocol Sentences. In *Logical positivism*, edited by A. J. Ayer. Glencoe (Ill): Free Press, pp. 199-208.
Peirce, C. S. (1958). *Charles S. Peirce: Selected Writings*. New York: Dover.
Quine, W.V. (1960). *Word and Object*. Cambridge (MA): MIT Press.

Films

La Classe Operaia va in Paradiso, Elio Perri, 1971, Italy
I Girasoli, Vittorio De Sica, 1970, Italy

CHAPTER NINE

THE CAMERA AS SPECULUM:
EXAMINING FEMALE CONSCIOUSNESS
IN *LOST IN TRANSLATION*,
USING THE THOUGHT OF LUCE IRIGARAY

LUCY BOLTON

Luce Irigaray is usually associated with her use morphological figurality, drawing on the realm of female genitalia and sexuality to create a possible way for women to think about themselves other than phallocratically. Irigaray is a "theorist of change":[147] she calls for the creation of a state of genuine sexual difference, in which men and women exist in a culture of two,[148] rather than a traditional male/female binarism which positivises the male. In order to achieve alterity, Irigaray says women need a female symbolic, including a female divine[149] and recognition of natural maternal genealogy.[150]

There are many other aspects of Irigaray's thought, as well as these notions of morphology and symbolism, which can be drawn upon when seeking to create and preserve a feminine syntax and which can inform and support a reading of film which foregrounds female consciousness. Through utilising the thoughts and strategies of Irigaray, it is possible to identify on-screen representations of female consciousness which may not initially appear exceptional. *Lost in Translation* (Sofia Coppola, 2003), presents something different with regard to female subjectivity, which becomes explicable and coherent when analysed in Irigarayan terms. The film provides space for the creation and preservation of alterity on the part of the lead female character, Charlotte, using language, the body, space, time and representations of her interiority. The spectator is invited into dialogue with Charlotte and the film's

---

[147] Whitford (1991), p. 15.
[148] 'You Who Will Never Be Mine', Irigaray (2004), pp. 8-12.
[149] 'The Redemption of Women', Irigaray (2004), pp. 150-164.
[150] 'The Neglect of Female Genealogies', Irigaray (1993b), pp. 15-22.

open, optimistic ending enables her future explorations to be the abiding focus of the film. It is this invitation into dialogue that the writings of Irigaray also offer as a means to engage in the process of creating a situation of genuine sexual difference. Through her style of critique, challenge, suggestion and proposal, Irigaray addresses the problem, as she sees it, of women's status in patriarchal society and the symbolic realm and the challenge of creating the conditions in which change can take place.

The objectification of women in film, and the way in which female spectators relate to these objectified women, has been a major preoccupation of feminist film theory, in particular since Laura Mulvey's groundbreaking article on visual pleasure and "the gaze" in 1975.[151] The fetishisation and/or punishment of women on screen is such a common feature of mainstream cinema that, although much debated and criticized, many of Mulvey's points remain relevant to today's cinema. There are of course many films that feature women in lead roles, with female-centred or focused narratives, which concern women's experiences and lifestyles. However, it is still rare to find a film in which a woman's subjectivity is the driving force of the narrative. Even if a female character is central to the narrative, it is highly unusual for the audience to be invited to share her point of view, to be concerned with her thoughts, observations, reactions and concerns.

Irigaray's analysis of the problem of the lack of sexual difference in Western society informs acutely our understanding of the reasons why female consciousness has failed to be represented on screen in any meaningful way.[152] The idea that women lack a female imaginary or symbolic provides a reason for the paucity of female cinematic imagery outside of the phallocratic treatments first exposed by Mulvey. Irigaray describes how;

> this fault, this deficiency, this 'hole', inevitably affords woman too few figurations, images, or representations by which to represent herself. It is not that she lacks some 'master signifier' or that none is imposed upon her, but rather that access to a signifying economy, to the coining of signifiers, is difficult or even impossible for her because she remains an outsider, herself (a) subject to their norms. She borrows signifiers but cannot make her mark, or re-mark upon them.[153]

The consequences for women may however extend beyond a lack of signification: Irigaray argues that the necessary and inevitable consequence of this exclusion is hysteria – "a latent but not actual psychosis, for want of a

---

[151] Mulvey (1989).
[152] 'The Blind Spot of an Old Dream of Symmetry' and 'Speculum', Irigaray (1985b).
[153] *Ibid.*, p. 71.

practical signifying system".[154] This lack of facility for self-expression may explain the apparent lack of motivation or occupation of Charlotte in *Lost in Translation*. Charlotte describes herself as being "stuck" – she is not socially or emotionally compatible with her husband, and yet has nothing else to do except to accompany him for his working trip to Tokyo. Although she graduated from Yale the previous year, she has not yet found an occupation that enables her to express herself honestly. She is currently acting simply as her husband's companion. Submitting to the masculine theory of the subject, it seems, equates with accepting the impossibility of a specifically feminine imaginary through which Charlotte could begin to form her own empowering identity. At first sight, therefore, Charlotte is a straightforward and limited character. This depiction is consistent with Irigaray's description of the historical representation of women:

> For centuries, woman has appeared as superficiality itself – save for the natural profundity which is in the service of love and, above all, in the service of maternity, that is, physical interiority. She has been considered fickle, capricious, the one to whom thought and interiority will always remain foreign. To make man come out of himself, to awaken him from his dreams, she is asked to attract him in the game of seduction and love.[155]

The result of this superficiality is a concentration on exteriority and a celebration of physical attributes, at the expense of complexity of character or interiority: "As a result, it seems that woman's garment becomes more important than her skin".[156] The destruction of this emphasis on exteriority is a challenge for cinema, not only because it is an industry in which female physical beauty is so highly prized, but also because the notion of the representation of interiority on screen is not straightforward. Irigaray provides a subtle approach to this problem: she calls for a movement away from masculine discourse and patriarchy and towards the creation of a female specificity.

> ...the female body is not to remain the object of men's discourse or their various arts but that it become the object of a female subjectivity experiencing and identifying itself. Such research attempts to suggest to women a morpho-logic that is appropriate to their bodies. It's aimed at the male subject, too, inviting him to redefine himself as a body with a view to exchanges between sexed subjects.[157]

---

[154] *Idem.*
[155] Irigaray (2000b), p. 58.
[156] *Idem.*
[157] Irigaray (2000a), p. 59.

Irigaray suggests strategies that women might employ in order to create a syntax of female subjectivity, many of which resonate with the visual realm of film. For example, when discussing how a woman might interpret a dream, Irigaray appeals for the recall of:

> those "pictures" made for children, pictographs in which the hunter and hunted, and their dramatic relationships, are to be discovered between the branches, made out from between the trees. From the spaces between the figures, or stand-in figures. Spaces that organize the scene, blanks that sub-tend the scene's structuration and that will yet not be read as such. Or not read at all? Not seen at all? Never in truth represented or representable, though this is not to say they have no effect upon the present scenography. But fixed in oblivion and waiting to come to life. Turning everything upside down and back to front.[158]

This is one of the features of the cinematography and visual style of *Lost in Translation* – it answers Irigaray's call to "jam(s) the theoretical machinery" with a "disruptive excess"[159] of detail, focus, sound and colour. There are several scenes which consist of Charlotte exploring the city around her. Charlotte is shown to be travelling on the underground, observing what people are reading on the train, then strolling through the gardens of a temple and observing the monks chanting. The camera lingers on her for several seconds as she watches the monks, and also studies the object of her interest. There are also several scenes which show Charlotte as a tiny figure against the backdrop of the vast, colourful and neon-drenched Tokyo cityscape. These scenes are not plot-driven or narrative advancing: they serve to represent the interior life of Charlotte and to enable us to share to some extent what she is thinking about and experiencing. On these occasions, the narrative is paused by the on-screen woman, but in complete contrast to the way in which Mulvey describes a woman's body freezes the narrative.[160] This is not the physical appearance of the woman being used as a spectacle, rather it is an invitation to consider the woman's mind. *Lost in Translation* is driven to a large extent by the subjective contemplations and motivations of its female lead character. These scenes take place in the "spaces between" which Irigaray asks women to identify,[161] and which are highlighted by an imitation of expected generic conventions.

Irigaray suggests mimesis as a means of operating outside a masculine tradition. In order to disrupt the patriarchal hierarchy and symbolic systems, Irigaray says, one must assume the feminine role deliberately – "to convert a

---

[158] *Ibid*, p. 138.
[159] 'The Power of Discourse', Irigaray (1985a), p. 78.
[160] Mulvey (1989), p. 19.
[161] Irigaray (2000a), p. 59.

form of subordination into an affirmation and thus begin to thwart it".[162] This is a way of understanding how *Lost in Translation* conveys its difference: it takes on an established genre with "stock" characters, an extra-marital romance between an older man and a younger woman, and does something very different and surprising with the female role. For example, the credits open with a picture of a girl's bottom lying on a bed wearing pink see-through panties. This is reminiscent of many similar body-shots of women on-screen, but perhaps most redolently the opening credits of *Pretty Woman* (1990), which show a woman's hips in skimpy briefs lying on a bed. That film of course goes on to be about the most stereotypical of all Hollywood women – the whore with a heart of gold, who secretly yearns respectability and ultimately is rescued by her Prince Charming. In *Lost in Translation* however, the pink-panty shot is overlaid with the film's title – an indication that this is not going to be a straightforward depiction of female sexuality (as the usual meanings of onscreen femininity are effectively "lost" in their translation into a new filmic mode which foregrounds female subjectivity). And it turns out to be far from the shallow stereotype one might have come to expect: the pants are worn by the lead character, who has a philosophy degree, is married, and is caught in the middle of an existential crisis.

It is useful to compare this with a classic romantic comedy involving a relationship between and older man and a younger woman, *The Seven Year Itch* (Billy Wilder, 1955). In this film, the body of "the girl", played by Marilyn Monroe, is consistently used to freeze the narrative; in the scene in which she is introduced, the male protagonist and the spectator view her from behind as she walks up the stairs carrying a fan; similarly in the iconic spectacle where she stands over the subway grating, her white dress billowing up around her waist. This "girl" has no name and is not shown to occupy any space of her own. There is no consideration of her subjectivity or point of view in the film: it is arguable that she does not exist at all outside of the man's imagination. By comparing *Lost in Translation* with this classic of the genre, the different filmic treatment of the woman becomes clear: the recent film is similar to but different from the classic, in important and meaningful ways. The conventions of narrative logic suggest a familiar reading, but re-read them and they show an alternative representation of the female. There is a gap – between what we expect to see in the context of the familiar generic conventions and what is portrayed on screen. It is in this gap that the different representation of the female can be located: not an alternative way of objectifying women, rather an alternative way of portraying their subjectivity.

---

[162] Irigaray (1985a), p. 76.

Irigaray rejects Lacan's mirror as flat and reflective of male narcissism,[163] and suggests a speculum instead, used as a light and a mirror, as a way of getting inside the female:

> to put into place a mode of specularization that allows for the relation of woman to "herself" and to her like. Which presupposes a curved mirror, but also one which is folded back on itself, with its impossible reappropriation "on the inside" of the mind, of thought, of subjectivity. Whence the intervention of the speculum and the concave mirror, which disturb the staging of representation according to too-exclusively masculine parameters.[164]

Lost in Translation suggests how the camera lens can be used in this mode of specularization, in a subversive technique of imitation of female images. It is not an attempt to define "woman", rather it is the forging of an opportunity of individual expression, and that individual character happens to be female. Irigaray is not attempting definition either,[165] rather she is seeking to locate another realm, in the unconscious and symbolic, where women can find expression. She asks "whether the feminine does not, in part, consist of what is operating in the name of the unconscious? Whether a certain 'specificity' of woman is not repressed/censured under cover of what is designated as the unconscious?"[166] This is important in analyzing the ways in which the films represent female consciousness using visual styles and techniques which are not always obviously gendered, for example Charlotte's explorations of places in Tokyo. As described above, these scenes are not about female experience – they are blanks in which the spectator is invited to be privy to the consciousness of the female character.

There are several other strategies proposed by Irigaray that are useful in terms of identifying gaps or spaces within the narrative in which female consciousness may be located. For example, according to Irigaray, woman no longer needs to subscribe to the ritual of courtly love, rather it,

> can be played out in language alone. One style is enough. One that pays its respects and attention to the gaps in speech, to the not-all in discourse, to the hollowness of the Other, to the half-said, even to the truth. Not without coquetry, seductions, intrigues, enigmas, and even …ejaculations – whose prematurity is more or less retarded by their passage into language – punctuating the movements of identification with the lady's pleasure.[167]

---

[163] Irigaray (1985b), p. 144; Irigaray (1985a), p. 154.
[164] 'Questions', Irigaray (1985a), pp. 154-5.
[165] *Ibid.*, pp. 122-127.
[166] *Ibid.*, p. 123.
[167] 'Cosi Fan Tutti', Irigaray (1985a), p. 104.

The way in which Charlotte and Bob relate to each other is played out along the lines Irigaray describes. There is no sexual intimacy between them, but they get to know each other and fall in love through ludic verbal wordplay and companionable silence. Their "affair" certainly contains coquetry and intrigues, but is not based on any discourse of courtly love or sexual cat-and-mouse. Unlike in The Seven Year Itch, there is no invitation to the spectator to share in an undercurrent of lascivious intent on the part of the older man; neither is the younger woman a manipulated ingénue who is at risk of being taken advantage of: the progressive relationship between Charlotte and Bob is an even-handed development between two equal individuals.

In exemplifying a place where a feminine syntax might be located, that is "a syntax that would make woman's self-affection possible",[168] Irigaray suggests that it might be, deciphered in the gestural code of women's bodies. But, since their gestures are often paralyzed, or part of the masquerade, in effect, they are often difficult to "read". Except for what resists or subsists "beyond". In suffering, but also in women's laughter. And again: in what they "dare" – do or say – when they are among themselves.[169]

Irigaray's writing on the gestural code of women's bodies is integral to reading the representation of Charlotte: in particular, the idea that girls might "keep the lips closed as a positive move".[170] Irigaray says that women find self-expression when their lips are touching and when their whole body is in movement; that a woman "is more at loss when she is still than when she is moving, because when fixed in one position she is a prisoner, open to attack in her own territory".[171] As a strategy, Irigaray suggests that women should,

> Insist also and deliberately upon those blanks in discourse which recall the places of her exclusion and which by their silent plasticity, ensure the cohesion, the articulation, the coherent expansion of established forms. Reinscribe them hither and thither as divergencies, otherwise and elsewhere than they are expected, in ellipses and eclipses that deconstruct the logical grid of the reader-writer.[172]

These strategies operate in relation to the ways in which Charlotte is shown to communicate with the world around her. Much of Charlotte's screen-time is spent silently wandering around Tokyo, exploring the city and observing its inhabitants. She is seen to pass through an amusement arcade, where the

---

[168] *Ibid.*, p. 132.
[169] *Ibid.*, p. 134.
[170] 'Gesture in Psychoanalysis', Irigaray (1993c), p. 100.
[171] *Ibid.*, p. 102.
[172] 'Any Theory of the Subject Has Always Been Appropriated by the Masculine', Irigaray (1985b), p. 142.

dancing and frolicking of local youngsters intrigues and amuses her. There is a lengthy scene where she wanders around the hotel, observing the inane platitudes of the actress, discovering women who are flower arranging and who invite her to arrange a flower herself. There is also a scene where Charlotte takes a train, listening to her headphones, and then observes a wedding procession. She skips over stepping stones in a pond and ties a piece of paper onto a tree covered in similar knots of paper. She is silent and non-responsive verbally, but is experimenting with other forms of communication, using gesture and motion. Charlotte tells Bob that in her search to find a way of expressing herself, she is trying writing and photography; Charlotte is evaluating her future as a writer, frustrated, she says, by the fact that she hates what she writes. She displays laughter or ridicule at the world around her, and although sometimes this laughter is shared with Bob, mostly her wry observations are kept to herself. Charlotte's amusement at Bob's appearance and behaviour serves to share her point of view with the audience and break down any status or superiority based on age or gender that Bob may otherwise have enjoyed, for example when she notices his feet looking ridiculous in hotel slippers. When Charlotte's husband meets the actress who is staying in the hotel under the name of Evelyn Waugh, the focus of the scene is Charlotte's reaction to their superficial conversation. Charlotte's expression reveals her amused disdain, which the spectator is invited to share through the pivotal way in which she is positioned.

Charlotte's individuality is emphasised by her plain clothes, hair and make-up. She toys with lipstick, putting up her hair and wearing a pink wig, but this masquerade can be seen as an attempt to disguise the difficulties she is having trying to find a way of expressing or defining herself. Mary Ann Doane describes how the masquerade, "in flaunting femininity, holds it at a distance".[173] The excess of femininity creates a distance between oneself and one's image, which Irigaray describes as a stage before self knowledge.

> The mirror signifies the constitution of a fabricated (female) other that I shall put forward as an instrument of seduction in my place. I seek to be seductive and to be content with images of which I theoretically remain the artisan, the artist. I have yet to unveil, unmask, or veil myself for me – to veil myself so as to achieve self-contemplation[174]

The analysis and strategies of Irigaray with their rich visual and linguistic imagery provide tools for reading the enigmatic representation of Charlotte in a way that accounts for the foregrounding of her interiority. The film's majestic and detailed imagery, pace and language, as well as the even footing of the male

---

[173] Doane (1999), p. 138.
[174] Irigaray (1993c), p. 65.

and female lead characters, create conditions for an exploration of female consciousness on screen. The portrayal of Charlotte is subtly revolutionary. Although the film may appear initially to be a star vehicle for Bill Murray, who plays Bob, the resonance of the film's ending lies in the fact that Charlotte has so many opportunities ahead of her and so much she may be able to achieve. It seems unlikely that Charlotte will stay with her husband or continue to be his companion, but the alternative is not presented as her leaving one man for another. The final exchange between Charlotte and Bob is inaudible to the spectator. This constitutes a marked "space between", which enables a meditation on Charlotte's future, as the accompanying soundtrack plays the Jesus and Mary Chain singing 'Listen to the girl, as she takes on half the world'.[175] The emphasis rests on what and how Charlotte herself can become.

---

[175] The Jesus and Mary Chain, 'Just Like Honey'.

References

Works by Luce Irigaray

This Sex Which Is Not One (New York: Cornell University Press, 1985a).
Speculum of the Other Woman (New York: Cornell University Press, 1985b).
An Ethics of Sexual Difference (London: Athlone, 1993a).
Je, tu, nous (London and New York: Routledge, 1993b).
Sexes and Genealogies (New York and Chichester: Columbia University Press, 1993c).
I Love to You, translated by Alison Martin (London and New York: Routledge, 1996).
Democracy Begins Between Two (London: Athlone, 2000a).
To Be Two (London and New York: Routledge, 2000b).
The Way of Love (London and New York: Continuum, 2002a).
Between East and West (New York and Chichester: Columbia University Press, 2002b).
Key Writings (London and New York: Continuum, 2004).

Other works

Doane, Mary Ann (1999). Film and the Masquerade: Theorising the Female Spectator. In *Feminist Film Theory: A Reader*, edited by Sue Thornham. Edinburgh: Edinburgh University Press.
Mulvey, Laura (1989). Visual Pleasure and Narrative Cinema, *Screen, 1975.* Reproduced in *Visual and Other Pleasures*. Hampshire and New York: Palgrave.
Whitford, Margaret (1991). *Philosophy in the Feminine*. London and New York: Routledge.
-- (2004). *The Irigaray Reader*. Oxford and Massachusetts: Blackwell Publishers.
-- and Morwenna Griffiths (eds.) (1988). *Feminist Perspectives in Philosophy.* Hampshire and London: The Macmillan press.

Films

Lost in Translation, Sophia Coppola, 2003, USA/Japan
The Seven Year Itch, Billy Wilder, 1955, USA

Music

'Just Like Honey', by The Jesus and Mary Chain, *Psychocandy*, 1999, Warner

CHAPTER TEN

PLATO'S CAVE AND THE BIG SCREEN

STEPHEN RAINEY

In what follows, I will discuss the nature of cinematic knowledge, addressing whether such a thing can exist. I begin with a discussion of knowledge *per se* and go on to discuss a plausible conception of what film is in relation to an audience. This discussion is linked to Plato's analogy of the cave, to be found in *The Republic* book seven. I then go on to highlight some points of contact and some parallels between cinema and the cave. Having put forward a general characterisation of what goes on when we are watching films, based in the discussion of Plato and the cave, I draw a cautious conclusion concerning cinematic knowledge.

> Behold! Human beings living in a underground den, which has a mouth open towards the light and reaching all along the den; here they have been from their childhood, and have their legs and necks chained so that they cannot move, and can only see before them, being prevented by the chains from turning round their heads. Above and behind them a fire is blazing at a distance, and between the fire and the prisoners there is a raised way; and you will see, if you look, a low wall built along the way, like the screen which marionette players have in front of them, over which they show the puppets.
> [...]
> And do you see... men passing along the wall carrying all sorts of vessels, and statues and figures of animals made of wood and stone and various materials, which appear over the wall? Some of them are talking, others silent.
> [...]
> Like ourselves [...] they see only their own shadows, or the shadows of one another, which the fire throws on the opposite wall of the cave?[176]

Plato's cave analogy is designed to make stark the contrast in platonic thought between the real and the unreal. For Plato, truth has to be eternal and unchanging. It has to fixed in a way opinion is not. This is a difference between

---

[176] Plato (1967), Book 7.

the real and the unreal for Plato; the unreal is fallible belief, while the real is eternal and unchanging truth. The real is true knowledge and is discovered through the intellect by means of reflection, and so is only available to those whose intellects are correctly ordered; available only to philosophers.

An example will serve to clarify. Imagine that we meet a person who stands six feet in height. We remark in description of them that they are tall. Next, we meet another person, standing seven feet in height. Again, in description, we remark that they are tall. Plato worries that in such a case as this, we are confused. On the one hand, we are saying that six feet is tall while on the other, we say that seven feet is tall. This looks like a contradiction;

Six feet = 'Tall'
Seven feet = 'Tall'
Therefore
Six feet = Seven feet

This is clearly wrong, and it is clear that the term "tall" cannot be defined once and for all with reference to any person, or anything, that we will meet in experience. As it is for "tall", so it is for all universal terms. Plato's diagnosis of this problem is that the reality we meet in experience is debased. It is only good for opinion, and opinion is not knowledge. Thus, those who talk of truth in terms of the world that they experience are radically mistaken and can never recover from their mistake. However, Plato does not suggest that knowledge is impossible; he is not a sceptic. We do know what we are talking about when we say that this or that thing is tall, it's just that the explanation cannot be found of this in the world of experience. The only other option, then, is in the world of the intellect. Thus, when we say that this or that thing is tall, we aren't saying that tallness is defined by naming these things, but rather we are discerning in things their participation in the form of tallness. The forms are intellectual realities for Plato and therefore only discoverable once and for all via an intellectual route.

So, in the cave analogy, the shadowplay on the wall of the cave represents the world of experience. It is a merely indistinct impression of the really real world which is represented by the light outside the mouth of the cave. Those prisoners, with their heads fixed facing forward, represent the average person, running through life content to say they know what they do based on the shadowplay. They are prisoners because they don't know that their world is merely shadows. Philosophers, having seen through the shadowplay, make a break for the outside, exchanging the firelight for the sun thus exchanging opinion for knowledge.

In appearance, the modern cinema theatre resembles Plato's cave; the huddled masses are transfixed by the flitting images cast against the wall of the otherwise darkened cavern. In import too, perhaps, the analogy holds; for many, cinema is escapism. Suspension of disbelief for a couple of hours entails treating the antics of the shadowplay as real until, reluctantly, we must drag ourselves back to real reality as the houselights go up and exchange the light of the projector for the light of the sun.

Of course for Plato, on this analogy, the world outside the cave is the really real world and to get there is a release. Whilst enchanted by the shadowplay, or the silver screen, we are in the servitude of desire and of mere belief, not in possession of knowledge. Such cognitive categories as desire and belief are available to all, hence form part of a world to be transcended, to be left behind. As far as Plato is concerned, there is Truth to be found, so we do ourselves a disservice if we are contented by these lesser attitudes. What's more, this eternal Truth can only be found by reflection; only by adhering to that which Reason alone delivers can we be safe in any claim. The world of perceptions, flitting and indistinct, is the diametric opposite to this, being temporary and fallible.

This last description of the world of the senses, that world which Plato believes must be overcome, is in fact the world we seem to seek today. Plato, through many of his dialogues, attempts to dialogically and inexorably draw the reader to a conclusion of, if not the absolute truth of his aim, at least the absolute falsity of some alternatives. "We" (defined in an appropriately woolly way) seem unhappy with the idea of absolutes *per se*. In fact, we generally see absolutism as opposed to dialogical exposition. The former smacks of imposition, of ensnarement, while the latter leaves one with the sense of freedom that seems comforting. We seem to like, nowadays, more elbow-room than Plato might allow us.

In film, however, we see things differently. Plato's escape from the cave is a liberation of the mind to ponder only that which is the case, fixed and true for eternity. This kind of position is often called an Archimedean point of view, recalling Archimedes' boast that with a long enough lever he could shift the whole world. This label, then, is supposed to suggest the extrinsicality of the Platonic point of view. Being "outside" the world is supposed to allow one to peer back without the sully of bias or interest, thus to apprehend the Truth.

In film, the audience might be seen in just this way. Think of an empty cinema running movies for eternity with no-one watching. As well as giving one a feeling of Sartrean nausea, or catalysing an existential moment perhaps, it should also be clear that the films will run their course without any viewers, thus the viewer is utterly extrinsic to the event. Thus, when the audience is presented with a showing, they might be supposed to be in the ideal Platonic or Archimedean point of view.

Immediately, however, this kind of talk in this context begins to sound odd. We rarely think of watching a film in the way Plato would conceive possible from the Archimedean point of view. We rarely say, when asked what a film was like, that it was 'true'. True to life, maybe, meaning realistic, but then it will be precisely a depiction of the sort of shadowplay the illusions of which Plato hopes to dispel. More likely, we would recommend a film based upon what it shows in a sense deeper than merely what is depicted in it and how realistically. The truth we would speak of in film would be the truth of the vagaries shown therein; the poignancy of a relationship, the pathos of a character, the humanity of a hero. When we notice such aspects as these in film, we are not pondering absolutes, paradigms of right reasoning, but the perhaps implicit interconnections among people and their circumstances. Again, what we seem to look for in a cinematic work is precisely the problematic stuff Plato's intellectual stance would rid us of.

On the one hand, then, Plato advocates as necessary the ascent to an ideal intellectual position from which eternal truth is apprehensible. The cinema audience seem related to film in just this radically extrinsical way. However, from this point of view, the on-screen antics seem irrelevant to the audience as the relevance of the content of film presents itself in a way which presupposes a connectedness that the Archimedean point of view is meant to overcome.

On the presupposition of an Archimedean point of view in philosophy, W. V. Quine has this to say:

> The philosopher's task differs from [other scientists'], then, in detail; but in no such drastic way as those suppose who imagine for the philosopher a vantage point outside the conceptual scheme that he takes in charge. There is no such cosmic exile. He cannot study and revise the fundamental conceptual scheme of science and common sense without having some conceptual scheme, whether the same or another no less in need of philosophical scrutiny, in which to work. He can scrutinize and improve the system from within, appealing to coherence and simplicity; but this is the theoretician's method generally[177]

Quine then is saying that it is only by assuming a connectedness with any matter that we can understand whether or not we agree with it. Even the critic of a point of view has to engage with that point of view on it's own terms, albeit with the hope of finding fault therein. Plato's ideal Cosmic Exile, then, is the product of a misconstrued hope. Should the philosopher of his analogy find his way out of the cave into the light of the sun, and should they then come back to liberate others, they would be stuck without the conceptual vocabulary of the cave-dwellers. Their liberation would fail if the philosopher-liberator couldn't make herself clear in terms understood by the enslaved; you can't paint a picture of the sun using shadows.

---

[177] Quine (1960), p. 275.

Of course, there would have to be some difference between philosopher and cave-dweller, or else upon re-entering the cave the philosopher would once more become transfixed by the shadows. The idea of communication between liberator and enslaved requires a point of conceptual contact, but this can not be assumed to be total in either direction; the philosopher can't just switch their point of view back to the cave-dwellers or else they would once more be subsumed by the shadows. Some asymmetry is required in order that difference can be maintained.

So it seems that the radically extrinsic point of view cannot be maintained as it requires a conceptual remove such that any bridging between categorial sets would be precluded. Neither, though, can some kind of gestalt switching[178] be postulated between categorial sets, as such radical switches would leave the chance of explanation between sets redundant. Thus, with the external and internal points of view in doubt, a liminal view must be advanced; liminal in the sense that the thresholds of conceptualisations can be understood as the limits of a point of view. Furthermore, the mind is broad enough to assume points of view on their own terms.

So for film, a liminal view means that, while the audience is utterly extrinsic to what the screen shows, their understanding of it nonetheless assumes the identification of the points of view embodied in characters and the significance *for them* of situations. Indeed, only upon such a liminal understanding can one explain how a single viewer can comprehend the breadth of films they do and in what detail; from Wim Wenders' angels in *Wings of Desire* and David Lynch's Psychic Special Agent in *Firewalk with Me*, to Wes Anderson's lovesick schoolboy in *Rushmore* and the intense personality of Colonel Kurtz in Coppola's *Apocalypse Now*. Such diversity could never be grasped in its full sense from one privileged point of view; the subtleties would, of necessity, be ignored. Nor could an absolute identification with every character who was written and every situation that arose be possible, or healthy for that matter.

The nature of reality in film is thus in the representation of alternative points of view such that their liminal nature can be comprehended. From the relative privacy of the cinema chair, then, the lesson can be learned that for any point of view, including those of the viewer, certain entailments and possibilities are ruled in, others ruled out. That, at the same time, all points of view are constrained and mutable.

Thus, the platonic cave of the movie theatre has its value precisely in its depiction of the shadowplay and the audience's self-consciously relative release when the house lights go up. It is the suspension of disbelief whilst in the cave

---

[178] A 'gestalt switch' is when one's perception of some image changes, as in the famous 'duck/rabbit' example.

of the movie theatre that gains cinematic knowledge, as opposed to the apprehension of the immutable and indubitable that for Plato is the mark of knowledge.

Now it might simply be denied that what I have termed "cinematic knowledge" is a distinct category of knowledge at all, that anything other than opinion will result even from the closest watching of any film. This brings us back to the point at which the discussion started, namely the definition of knowledge *per se*.

If, as I seem to be saying, knowledge is supposed to be defined widely enough so as to admit the sort of things one can come to believe by watching films, then it might seem that I have identified knowledge with belief. Worse, in fact, I would seem have identified knowledge with hypothetical belief as I have plugged the apprehension of the opinions of pretend people in fictional scenarios into the concept of knowledge. Were this the case, I would seem to suggest that whatever one believed, one was entitled to refer to it as knowledge. It doesn't take much to realise the deficiency of such a definition of knowledge; there is no chance of error if any old belief I have is knowledge.

It seems clear to me that part of the concept of knowledge is that it is different from error. Without the possibility of error, there is no chance of knowledge, in fact. So I have to show how my asserted position is not simply the identification of opinion with knowledge.

Due to the untenable nature of the Platonic point of Cosmic Exile, as pointed out in the quotation from Quine and hinted at throughout, knowledge cannot be defined as the grasping of some extrinsic really real reality. The separation between belief and knowledge required by such a definition robs one of the conceptual contact necessary to talk of what is claimed to be known. The necessity of conceptual contact and the ability to discuss what is known are therefore constraints upon what knowledge is. In terms of points of view, conceptual contact is cashed out as understanding another's predicament, though one may not share their circumstances. The ability to discuss supposed knowledge is cashed out similarly as being, at least in principle, capable of describing the predicament to another. This is intended as a minimal set of constraints upon knowledge, meaning that *whatever else* knowledge might be, it *must be* identifiable and describable. Wittgenstein, in his *Philosophical Investigations* can be read as putting a similar constraint upon what will pass for knowledge with the words, "A nothing will do as well as a something about which nothing can be said".[179]

Since I have supposed film to be the liminal depiction of points of view, and the watching of films to be the apprehension of these points of view, it follows

---

[179] Wittgenstein (1958) §304.

that these two constraints are respected by film. Watching a film requires that the viewer understand what is going on; in the simplest terms, one understands that circumstances are swaying characters in certain ways and that these characters are forced to act or refrain from acting along certain limited lines. Being able to describe what goes on amounts to, at least, being able to discern why and how these limits upon action are present for these characters in these circumstances. Thus, it seems that what results from the watching of films is a something as opposed to a nothing.

The presence of disagreement among critics and audiences regarding the import of a film also points to the reality of cinematic knowledge. For the very notion of a disagreement presupposes that reasons exist for and against some description or analysis. Thus, an intelligent debate about whether, say, Darren Aronofsky's *Pi* is a story of one man's descent into madness, or a deeper insight into the conflict between free will and determinism, or chaos and order, will be characterised by each party in the debate having reasons for what they assert. In other words, the claims that can be made about the nature of cinematic reality have an epistemological status.

Thus, I conclude with a somewhat negative strategy; I suppose cinematic knowledge to be real owing to its fulfilment of two very minimal constraints upon knowledge, and owing to its aptness for genuine debate. While this may not prove that cinematic knowledge is really knowledge, it does shift the burden of proof to the sceptic. In other words, I have shown the parallel between ordinary knowledge and that derived from film; it is up to the sceptic to characterise the asymmetry.

References

Plato (1961). The Republic. In *The Collected dialogues of Plato*, E. Hamilton and H. Cairns (eds.). Princeton: Princeton University Press.

Quine, W. V. O. (1960). *Word and Object*. Cambridge (MA): MIT Press.

Wittgenstein, L. (1958). *Philosophical Investigations*. G. E. M Anscombe (tr. and ed.). Oxford: Blackwell.

AFTERWORD

DES O'RAWE

The publication of this collection of papers represents a valuable contribution to contemporary studies in the relations between philosophy and film. Inevitably, difficult questions arise for the philosopher who seeks an intellectually productive encounter with film images and film culture, and *From Plato's Cave to the Multiplex* is rich in arguments and ideas that address many of these difficulties, bestowing further respectability on the once scandalous relationship between philosophy and films.

While 'continental philosophy' has an impressive tradition of involvement in debates about the ontological, phenomenological, hermeneutic, and aesthetic aspects of film-making and film appreciation, it is really only in recent times that philosophers from elsewhere have begun to carefully delineate the philosophical contours of cinema. Various reasons can be offered to explain their reluctance to regard the cinema as an art form capable of informing philosophy about the nature of reality, perception, interpretation, and beauty, not least of which is the fact that Film Studies has often done little to make itself attractive to them.

Traditionally, Anglo-American Film Studies has been drawn towards obtuse semiotic and dubious psychoanalytical modes of analysis, regarding an aversion to analytical questions about filmic forms and structures as a cardinal virtue rather than a fatal flaw. Wittgenstein may have sought refuge from the impossibility of philosophy by going to watch Ginger, Fred and Betty Grable but film theoreticians are not given to seeking out the *Tractatus* as an antidote to the enticing generalities of this or that theory of culture. Instead, throughout the 1970s and 1980s, countless film and media studies conferences, journal articles, and books congratulated themselves on being able to speculate on the ways in which 'film' (which suddenly came to include T.V. advertisements, chat shows, cartoons, and *Top of the Pops*) represented social relations and reproduced ideology. Incantations to the tune of 'the medium is the message' reverberated through the empty corridors of a discourse that had little interest in the aesthetic particularities of film, let alone their philosophical import. Meanwhile, philosophers, many of whom had now withdrawn to the Games Room of language, were not in the mood to be interrupted by questions such as: Does the cinema involve itself in philosophical activity? Do films think? Do its forms, structures, and narrative situations relate in any meaningful way to the language and arguments of philosophy?

Despite this impasse, however, certain philosophers – most notably, Stanley Cavell and Noël Carroll – did create new comparative contexts for the study of philosophy and film, and the growth of this area of enquiry within the fields of both Film Studies and Philosophy is due in no small part to their perseverance. Today, philosophical approaches to the study of the cinema are no longer confined to French intellectuals who have always been able to locate in the cinema an array of philosophical implications and possibilities. Recent work by figures such as Murray Smith, Gregory Currie, Sarah Cooper, Stephen Mulhall, Richard Kearney, Irving Singer, David Rodowick, and Daniel Frampton (who has even coined the term, 'filmosophy') indicates a significant shift towards a more thorough study of the philosophical dimensions of film. Furthermore, given that some of the most philosophically sophisticated writing on the cinema today is being produced by Francophone writers – such as Nicole Brenez, Raymond Bellour, and Jacques Rancière – the continued caricaturing of so-called 'French theory' by parochial American ('post-theory') academics is unjustified. Despite these developments, however, there is still a danger that having sobered up after its structuralist excesses, Anglo-American Film Studies is now becoming increasingly intoxicated by large, undiluted measures of Gilles Deleuze and Slavjo Žižek. Indeed, what may prove most useful about the new willingness of contemporary philosophers to participate in the study of film will be their ability to lend some analytical clarity to a discipline that still has a habit of diving headfirst into the shallow end of critical theory.

This is not to say that graduate students should completely disregard the film-related writings of Deleuze and Žižek. Deleuze, for example, has developed philosophical concepts that are relevant to a serious 'philosophy of film', particularly in his application of Bergsonian notions of memory, time, and duration to an understanding of the cinematic image, an application that is often sensitive to shot structures, montage variations, and framing issues. On the other hand, his idiosyncratic use of Peirceian semiotics is generally more trouble than it is worth: the suggestive in Deleuze is more instructive than the systematic. More playful in its references to the cinema, Žižek's approach is also not without its merits (i.e. its playfulness) and its unusual 'projections' at least familiarize us with a theoretical model that we can either defend or denounce (i.e. his re-reading of Lacan's re-reading of Freud). To his credit, Žižek has always been candid about his indifference to film aesthetics, and consistent in his rejection of any philosophy of film meaning and reception that wants to gloss over the essential obtrusiveness of subjectivity: sit back, relax and enjoy your symptom.

While Deleuze is content to elevate certain directors and their films to the status of philosophers and philosophical texts, the question 'What is cinema?' is of subsidiary importance to his more abiding concern, 'What is Philosophy?'. Similarly, for Žižek, the only question that matters is 'What (or where or when) is the Real?' rather than 'What (or how or when) do films communicate philosophically?'. Unexamined, Anglo-American Film Studies will doubtless fetishize these and other novel 'theories' and contrive ways of yoking them to particular films, themes, and cultural issues. However, a Film Studies that is informed by the rigors and rhetoric of philosophical argument is better placed to address the fact that a good film matters not because it illustrates a philosophical position but because it is a work of art.

Appropriations of the cinema in this way are not merely opportunistic; they fail to grasp (or wish to fail to grasp) the fact that art is always more important than its interpretations. If a philosopher wants to use a film to illustrate an argument or an issue, the film will always oblige because the philosopher is as adept as anyone else in seeing only what they want to see. What they then see may not be philosophically available. I would like to end this brief Afterword with a moment from the cinema that can also be a message to contemporary philosophy from the cinema:

> **Nana:**   Why do people have to say words to live?
> **Parain:** Expressing is to catch a moment of thinking. But
>   to say something you really want to say, you must
>   experience a life without words.
>   *Vivre sa vie* (Jean-Luc Godard, 1962)

CONTRIBUTORS

John Adams is researching Wittgensteinian philosophy of religion at the University of Liverpool. He has been interested in film for over two decades. Each year he teaches a philosophy of film course and regularly shows films in the philosophy department. His other interests include travel, religion, literature and the arts in general.

Lucy Bolton obtained a first class degree in Theology from the University of Nottingham and went on to undertake a Diploma in Law conversion course at City University. Lucy was called to the Bar of England and Wales in 1994 and practised criminal and family law until 2000, when she left the Bar to study for a Masters in Film Studies at Westminster University. Lucy's AHRC-funded research is concerned with developing a reading method for analysing the on-screen representation of female consciousness. She is drawing on Luce Irigaray's work to identify a mode of symbolic representation which can be read in the non-standard treatments of the female characters in three recent films directed by women: *Lost in Translation, In the Cut* and *Morvern Callar*. These recent films are compared with classic Hollywood films (*The Seven Year Itch, Klute* and *Marnie*), in order to highlight the manner and form of the differences in representation of the female.

John F. Catherwood is Lecturer in Applied Ethics in the School Of Politics, International Studies and Philosophy, at the Queen's University of Belfast. John is particularly interested in torture (and developing arguments to suggest that it is always wrong), the evaluative use of the term "person" and has recently published articles on the ethics of smoking (tobacco), and against the use of slippery slope arguments. Earlier publications and his doctoral thesis were on the topic of brain death, which was a real conversation stopper at parties.

G. B. Hill has earned the B.A. in English and Comparative Religion at Tufts University, the M.A. in Religion at Yale University, the M.A. in Liberal and Cultural Studies at Dartmouth College, and is currently a graduate student at the University of New Hampshire. His work ranges from the history of Western Christianity to twentieth-century American fiction and film. He has written on captivity narratives in early America, F. Scott Fitzgerald, and film. Throughout his scholarly work he focuses particularly on questions surrounding subjective, cultural, ethnic, and national identities. His current work focuses on twentieth-century American fiction and film and tropes of identity, especially those of racial and national performance and their intersection with modernism.

Mark C. Rainey obtained his BA in philosophy from Stirling University, where he is currently actively pursuing the further qualification of Mlit in Knowledge and Mind. His philosophical views on film have appeared in several online journals such as *CinemaScope* and he has given his views on philosophy and film at academic conferences.

Stephen Rainey obtained a first class degree and MA with distinction in philosophy from Queen's University Belfast, where he remains to this day, writing his PhD thesis on a contemporary view of rationality by Kantian means. He has previously edited a collection of philosophical papers entitled *Noesis*, published by Cambridge Scholars Press.

Orna Raviv holds a Bachelor's Degree in Cinema (1987), and is about to completing MA degree in Philosophy at Tel Aviv University. She received a grant for excellence from the faculty (2004), and is presently writing her master's thesis entitled "The Face and the Close-Up: Cinematic Thought in the Light of the Philosophy of Emmanuel Levinas", advised by Dr. Hagi Kenaan. Orna is a director and producer of fictional and documentary films. In the course of her work she has written, directed, and produced a full-length movie (1996), produced a documentary for the European National Geographic channel (2002), and a documentary for the Israeli Channel 2 television network.

Barbara Gabriella Renzi is completing her PhD on Scientific Methodology and Evolutionary Biology at the Queen's University of Belfast. She studied Philosophy of Science and specialised in Bioethics at the university 'La Sapienza' in Rome. She recently published "Natural Selection, Exaptation and the Evolution of Science" in *Philosophical Writings* and has previously co-edited a collection of philosophical papers entitled *Noesis*, published by Cambridge Scholars Press. Her poems appear in Italian anthologies.

Jolynna Sinanan studied her Bachelor of Creative Arts at the University of Melbourne, majoring in Media Studies and Creative Writing before receiving a scholarship to undertake her Honours in Film Studies as part of her Bachelor of Arts degree from the Australian National University in Canberra. She currently works between Melbourne and Phnom Penh as an English teacher and education consultant, developing the use of media methods in foreign language teaching.

Catherine Wheatley graduated from Oxford University with a first class degree in Modern Languages. She earned an M.A. in European Cinema at the University of Bath, before returning to Oxford, where she is at present a doctoral candidate in the Department of Medieval and Modern Languages. Catherine is particularly interested in questions of ethics and film, and her doctoral research, in which she focuses primarily on the films of Michael Haneke, is concerned with theorising the spectator's relationship to the cinematic image in terms of ethical philosophy. She has published articles on Michael Haneke, the philosophy of Gilles Deleuze and on film and ethics, and most recently on the emerging sub-genre of European 'post-pornography'. She has also several contributed entries to the *Routledge Encyclopedia of Documentary Film*.

INDEX OF NAMES AND FILMS